Napoleon Hill's Cookbook for Life

The Magic Ingredients of Success

Napoleon Hill
Judith Williamson

Copyright © 2007
The Napoleon Hill Foundation
All Rights Reserved

ISBN: 978-1-937641-13-9

Napoleon Hill World Learning Center
Purdue University Calumet
2300 173rd Street
Hammond, IN 46323
Email: nhf@purduecal.edu

The Napoleon Hill Foundation
University of Virginia-Wise
PO Box 1277
Wise, VA 24293
Website: www.naphill.org
Email: napoleonhill@uvawise.edu

Edited by Judith Williamson and Chris Lake
Cover Design by Uriel "Chino" Martinez
Production Assistance by Guang "Alan" Chen

Contents

Introduction i

1. Definiteness of Purpose 1
2. Mastermind Alliance 9
3. Applied Faith 17
4. Going The Extra Mile 29
5. Pleasing Personality 39
6. Personal Initiative 45
7. Positive Mental Attitude 51
8. Enthusiasm 61
9. Self-Discipline 69
10. Accurate Thinking 75
11. Controlled Attention 79
12. Teamwork 85
13. Learning from Adversity and Defeat 91
14. Creative Vision 101
15. Maintenance of Sound Health 107
16. Budgeting Time and Money 113
17. Cosmic Habitforce 119

Contributors 131

Napoleon Hill

SUCCESS COMPACT

This
Mastermind Alliance
Recognizes

_____

To Whom

Napoleon Hill

grants the privilege of being served by his personal guides who operate on the higher levels of intelligence, the names and the services to be rendered by each being as follows:

Prince of Hope to keep the future enriched with the promise of success and abundance. **Prince of Faith** to provide direct contact with infinite intelligence. **Prince of Love** to keep both body and mind youthful regardless of the passing years. **Prince of Sound Health** to keep the physical body healed and efficient at all times. **Prince of Prosperity** to provide all the money and opportunity for success that is needed. **Prince of Peace of Mind** to keep the mind free from all forms of fear and causes of worry. **Prince of Romance** to give joy and enthusiasm to every thought and every deed. **Prince of Patience** to provide self-discipline sufficient to meet all circumstances with a positive mental attitude. **Prince of Over-All Wisdom** to keep the other eight Princes eternally active in behalf of the makers of this compact.

I hereby gratefully accept the services of the nine invisible Princes and promise to express my gratitude to them each day.

_____   _____
Signed   Countersigned by

Introduction

This cookbook is meant to be fun and innovative as well as educational. It is a crossover book that serves two purposes: 1) to give the reader immediate access to the wholesome wisdom of Napoleon Hill and his Philosophy of Success, and 2) to share testimonials and favorite recipes of individuals who have used Dr. Hill's system to enhance all aspects of their lives. The men and women who appear in this ***Cookbook for Life*** have experienced many or all of the 17 Success Principles, and have benefited from them. These are ordinary people who, because of their firm belief, persistence, and creativity have done great things with their lives. They are not the type to sit back and whittle away their time watching the world go by without their input. They are doers and creators of their universe. Their testimonials and recipes ring true because they are written in their own words and directly from their own hearts. The old adage reminds us that "the proof is in the pudding." Our recipe contributors are certainly a "proven" commodity that you can personally use as a touchstone, guiding light, or signpost to your success.

Cooking is a creative art. It is also a cultural art. Recipes are procured from our personal past, our nation's past, and even our immediate, daily lives. Food shared is food remembered, and like a success philosophy, it has to be more than an armchair experience. It must be put to the test. The yeast must be proofed, the bread baked, the rice fried, the salad marinated, the beef boiled, and the chicken stir fried in order to get the intended result. Within families, favorite recipes are elevated to a sacred status. That special soup we remember from our childhood, or the way mom prepared chicken for Sunday dinner after church, not only tantalizes our taste buds but arouses our memory of the occasion during which the food was served. This imprinting heightens our awareness and locks in that personal story that is unique to each of us. Likewise, success recipes, when handed down through others take on a sacred, spiritual role as well. When people look out for each other's wellbeing, both are enriched. Sharing food enriches the body while sharing a universal success philosophy can enrich the soul and feed our inner self. See how the two go hand in hand?

Now, it is your turn. First, read this book in a cursory fashion skipping through the pages quickly. Next, hone in on a recipe and testimony that services your wellbeing and your life at this moment. Believe in synchronicity. Pause a little longer and read the recipe and testimony more slowly along with the explanation of the principle at the beginning of the chapter. Make the recipe and serve it to family and friends. Sense the overall feeling of whatever principle is being taught, and make some side notes in a cookbook journal that record your experience and learning. Finally, why don't you become a contributor to our next edition? At the back of this book is the same page that was sent as an invitation to each contributor. Fifty-five practitioners of Hill's philosophy said yes, and have made the difference for you by sharing something memorable and unique in our first edition. Can't you take a moment now and do the same? Remember, what you write down, lives forever. Give yourself the gift of immortality by recording your memories and advice. Write it down, do it now, share your wealth, and feel the richness of your gift giving both now and for "future generations not yet born," as Dr. Hill would add.

Looking forward to meeting you in our next edition.

To Your Success,

Judith Williamson

Judy Williamson

Director, Napoleon Hill World Learning Center

at Purdue University Calumet

My Recipe for Success

"That which you think today becomes that which you are tomorrow."

Napoleon Hill with *Think and Grow Rich*

1. Definiteness of Purpose

It has been said more than once that ***Definiteness of Purpose*** is the starting point of all achievement. If our journey is going to end at a specific destination, we must know that destination in advance. This sounds obvious when stated, but it is the most difficult step for 98/100 people to put into action. Knowing where you are going requires many life skills, personal foresight or vision, as well as applied faith. Finally, conditioning the subconscious mind to take over our goals is the key to releasing the power within us which makes possible the fulfillment of our plan and the arrival at our chosen destination. Just thinking about all this can make one hungry. It has been said too, that life is not about the destination, but the journey. As we all journey through life, I am reminded of one of my family's recipes that is worthy of sharing. It is Lone Ranger Soup. As a child, when I asked where this soup's name came from, my father would just say that it was named after the Lone Ranger who made this soup on the trail with Tonto, his Indian guide. My father said he knew this for certain, because he traveled with them…so much for family stories. As an adult, I now read the Stone Soup story to my classes at Purdue University Calumet. It too reminds me of the Lone Ranger Soup that my father frequently teased me about. As we all know, a good vegetable soup recipe is in every family's cookbook. Here's my family's below.

— Judith Williamson

Lone Ranger Soup
(Vegetable Beef Soup)

- salt to taste
- pepper to taste
- 3-4 T. chopped parsley, or to taste
- two cloves minced garlic, or to taste
- 3 to 4 lb. chuck roast with some fat
- 6 stalks celery, chopped
- 2-3 parsnips, chopped
- 1 large onion, chopped
- 6 carrots, chopped
- 1 small head of cabbage, sliced
- 2-3 potatoes cut small
- 1 can stewed tomatoes
- 1 large can tomato juice
- 2/3 c. rice
- 6 oz. noodles
- 1 c. frozen peas
- 1 c. frozen corn

Cook meat with salt, pepper, minced garlic, parsley, celery, chopped onion, carrots, and parsnips together in enough water to cover until tender. Add more water as needed. Simmer for approximately 1 to 1½ hours. Add potatoes, tomato juice, stewed tomatoes, rice, noodles, peas and corn. Simmer an additional 20 minutes. Adjust liquid to make a nice broth. Add cabbage and simmer 15 more minutes. Allow soup to boil, and finally add dumplings dropped by rounded teaspoonfuls into hot soup. Cook covered on low heat for an additional 15 minutes. Do not remove cover during final cooking. Dumplings will be thoroughly cooked if you follow the above directions.

Dumplings:

- 2 c. flour
- 5 eggs separated
- 1 T. butter
- 1/3 cup milk plus additional milk

In a large heavy saucepan place two cups of flour. Separate eggs. Whites in one cup, yolks in another. In the cup with the egg whites, add enough milk to make one cup. Next, ready an additional 1/3 c. more milk. Add egg whites with milk, additional milk, and butter to flour. Mix together and cook stirring constantly over low heat until mixture forms a ball. Do not allow the dough to stick to pan. Let cool. When cool, add egg yolks. Last 15 minutes that soup is cooking, drop dough by rounded teaspoonfuls into boiling soup. Cover, and let boil over low heat for 15 minutes.

Note: Dumpling recipe does not double well. If you want more dumplings, you will have to make the recipe two separate times in two separate pots.

This recipe makes a very good soup that the Lone Ranger perfected on the trail.

And, for dessert, another family favorite, Icebox Cheese Cake.

Definiteness of Purpose

> " ...the starting point of all achievement. "
> -Napoleon Hill

Recipe for Success

The Five Fundamental Steps to Success

There are five fundamental steps which must be taken by all who succeed.

They are:

1. Choice of a definite goal to be attained.
2. Development of sufficient power to attain one's goal.
3. Perfection of a practical plan for attaining one's goal.
4. Accumulation of specialized knowledge necessary for the attainment of one's goal.
5. Persistence in carrying out the plan.

Recipe for a Definite Major Purpose

Working with definiteness of purpose toward a single goal has many advantages, among them the following:

First: Singleness of purpose forces one to specialize and specialization tends toward perfection.

Second: A definite goal permits one to develop the capacity to reach decisions quickly and firmly.

Third: Definiteness of purpose enables one to master the habit of procrastination.

Fourth: Definiteness of purpose saves the time and energy one would otherwise waste while wavering between two or more possible courses of action.

Fifth: A definite purpose serves as a road-map which charts the direct route to the end of one's journey.

Sixth: Definiteness of purpose fixes one's habits so that they are taken over by the sub-conscious mind and used as a motivating force (involuntarily) in driving toward one's goals.

Icebox Cheese Cake – Old Fashioned
(Make the day before serving!)

1 stick margarine
2 pkg. graham crackers crumbled
2 T. sugar

Mix together and press into square glass dish
(Leave 1/8 c. of crumbled graham crackers for top of cake.)

1 pkg. jello (any flavor, but lemon works well)
½ c. boiling water

Dissolve the jello in the boiling water.

½ cup fruit juice (apple, cherry, etc.)
Add fruit juice to the jello mixture and let stand until lukewarm

1 lg. can chilled Milnot
2 T. sugar
1 large pkg. cream cheese at room temperature
1 c. sugar
2 tsp. vanilla

Beat chilled Milnot with the sugar until stiff. Separately, beat the cream cheese with one c. sugar and 2 tsp. vanilla.

Pour jello mixture into the Milnot mixture and beat again. Fold in the cream cheese mixture. Chill. Garnish with graham cracker crumbs, pecans and pineapple on top if desired prior to serving.

Note: This recipe is just like grandma used to make. Enjoy! It won't last in the refrigerator very long.

S.M.A.R.T.E.R. Than You Think

There were many times in my career as a psychotherapist when I have had to deal with issues of finding a "purpose" in life for others, let alone establishing a definiteness-of-purpose path for that individual. The one leads to the other with a simple formula embedded in any action plan. It is a formula that has kept thousands of my clients, and I am no exception, steadfast on their chosen paths.

It is a S.M.A.R.T.E.R. rule that when applied against any goal, immeasurably strengthens your resolve and your "Purpose." First understand that a purpose is NOT a destination. It's more like a direction, North, South, East, West, and your goals are various destination points along that direction. Then apply the SMARTER rule to each goal;

S is for specific: Clarity enhances definitiveness.
M is for measurable: Quantifiability is a gauge.
A is for achievable: Can ANYONE do this thing?
R is for realistic: Can YOU do this thing?
T is for timed: Set a completion date.
E is for enthusiasm: This leads to energy & power.
R is for relevance: Will this impact YOUR life?

Keeping these foremost in your consciousness will help you cut through your goals like a hot knife through butter. Your purpose and resolve then has a gauge to keep burning, much like the fuel indicator in your vehicle to Success. Happy journeys!

— Dr. Mel Gill

African Prawn Salad

1 pound prawns frozen, fully cooked, thawed
1 medium red onion thinly sliced
4 cups watermelon roughly chopped
2 jalapeño peppers, seeded, finely chopped
2 avocados roughly chopped
1 lime, juiced
1 teaspoon honey
3 tablespoons olive oil
3/4 (three quarter) teaspoon salt
1/4 (one quarter) teaspoon black pepper
1/2 cup coriander sprigs roughly chopped
1 clove of garlic finely chopped

1. In a large bowl, combine the prawns, jalapeños, avocados, onions and watermelons.
2. In a small bowl, whisk together the lime juice, honey, salt, pepper, garlic and oil.
3. Pour vinaigrette over the salad and toss. Add the coriander sprigs on the top. Set aside for 10 minutes for the flavours to meld.

This simple recipe characterizes for the Africans a long held cultural belief that Life is like the salad, a combination of specific, but separate quantifiable ingredients from the land, the sea, and the sun (our environment). In combination within a "recipe," the results are always the same.....nourishment for the Soul! Enjoy the Path! Enjoy the Sun!

I am, after all is said and done (Usually more said than done!), a Teacher. My path is singular and has never wavered in the past 35 years. I am here to help as many people as possible find, Truth, Meaning, Purpose, Hope, and Happiness. I have used various modalities, occupations, writings, radio and television to make this happen. I have only just begun. When I end, I wish to leave no trace except the many hearts I have touched, that are aflutter with possibilities and power!

A Purposeful Lifetime Relationship with Wealth

When baking bread, fresh yeast must be used or the dough won't rise. Dough rising is a critical step; let the process go too long and you won't have any bread.

Failing to plan your finances is no different; failing in this step, you could find yourself with no dough too. Think of investing as a recipe for bread. Throwing a bunch of investments into a bowl and hoping for the best is akin to shopping for ingredients without a recipe! Be clear about what you want to make before you begin. Where are you headed and what will it take to get there?

The ingredients for your recipe begin with Definiteness of Purpose. Behind purpose, your mastermind is critical, but only after you decide what you want to eat. Executive chefs use their team for prep work so they can focus on the big picture. An effective financial mastermind will help you to plan a "financial menu" around your tastes, shop for the ingredients, and help execute the recipe for you.

True wealth comes from living a purposeful life and money is a means to an end, not the end. Napoleon Hill was the inspiration behind my business slogan: "Wealth follows persistence and commitment to vision." Recipes begin with a vision.

—RICHARD J. KRASNEY, CFP

Passion Fruit Syrup

The basic fruit syrup is used by top chefs the world over to dress up the appearance and taste of any dessert. This recipe can be adapted to include your favorite fruit and you will find that the possibilities are limited only by the use of your imagination!

- 4 large passion fruit
- 1 lime
- 1/2 cup granulated sugar
- 1/4 cup water
- 1 tablespoon vanilla extract
- 1/4 cup dark rum (optional)

Halve passion fruits and scoop out pulp into a sieve. Rub through the sieve with a spoon to separate juice and seeds. Discard seeds. Juice lime through the sieve. Set aside pulp/juice mixture.

In a small saucepan, mix sugar, water, vanilla, and rum, and stir to dissolve. Bring to a boil and boil for 5 to 7 minutes or until mixture resembles a maple syrup consistency. Add passion fruit juice mixture, return to boil, and boil for 1 minute.

To sterilize for storage (optional): pour into small, hot, sterilized bottles and seal while hot. Put into a boiling water bath for 10 minutes.

Think and Grow Rich *was my "a-ha" moment. I realized my passion for helping others was my secret to happiness and that I exist to make a difference in the world. I redesigned my career and life in pursuit of my purpose. As president of RJK Wealth Management, I act as a "Personal CFO," helping clients define and align their purpose with their wealth. Now, I see my work as a contribution to society, because by helping people manage their wealth and make smarter decisions with their money, they can focus on making an impact on society.*

DEFINITENESS OF PURPOSE

Believe and You Shall Receive!

As Dr. Hill says, "believe and you shall receive." I always believed that I would one day skate with the Ice Capades. There was no doubt in my mind. There existed only that burning desire that is a key ingredient in any recipe for success. Here is my success recipe as it relates to Definiteness of Purpose:

1. Dream and dream big!
2. Believe in yourself. Adopt the "I can/will attitude."
3. Find the joy, passion, and that burning desire from within.
4. When you fall down, pick yourself up, and try again.
5. Enlist the help of others. Get a great coach!
6. Find the balance in life; physically, emotionally, and spiritually.
7. Spend your time and money wisely. We all get 24 hours to our day. What do you do with yours?
8. Laugh, and laugh loudly!
9. Have fun!
10. The journey is just as important as the final destination, so enjoy the ride!

And remember: dreams really do come true!

—ROBIN J. UPTON

Aunt Ruthie's Yummy Blueberry Cake

1 pint blueberries
6 tablespoons butter or margarine
1 1/4 cup granulated sugar
2 eggs, slightly beaten
2 cups flour
2 teaspoons baking powder
1/4 teaspoon salt
1/2 cup milk

Topping:
3 teaspoons sugar
1/2 teaspoon nutmeg

Preheat oven to 350 degrees.

Wash and drain berries well. Spread on paper towels to dry.

Cream butter and sugar. Add slightly beaten eggs.

Sift flour, baking powder, and salt.

Combine half the flour and half the milk. Mix well. Add remaining flour and milk. Mix well.

Fold in blueberries. It is important the berries are dry.

At this point, batter should be firm. Spread batter in greased 9-inch square pan.

Sprinkle topping on batter, then put in oven.

Bake 50–55 minutes, testing for doneness with toothpick or skewer. Cool well before removing from pan.

Enjoy with a nice cup of tea!

It was a tradition that every year on New Year's Eve, our family would trek into Boston to enter into a world of fantasy and delight. As that innocent four-year-old, I remember sitting in the audience of Boston Garden, mesmerized by the sparkling costumes, the shimmering lights, the melodic orchestra, and the talented skaters gliding effortlessly across the frozen stage—what a feast for the senses! I would sit there in awe and think to myself, "One day I'm going to do that." Little did I know, at the tender age of four, what it would truly take to become one of those beautiful Ice Capettes gliding across that frozen stage.

Just One More Sunset

As mentor to Donna Jones, young, vivacious, and number one salesperson for Kodak, it was a joy for me to watch her career explode with success until tragedy struck on a frozen lake in Montana in 1985. A traumatic head injury from a snowmobile accident rendered Donna unconscious for 48 days. The medical community gave up on her. Her family was devastated and began arrangements to warehouse her for life. As her friend and mentor, I asked that the family give her to me for one year to see if I could make a difference. I wanted Donna to enjoy one more sunset, a sight she cherished.

Having read *Think and Grow Rich* 25 years earlier and living by Napoleon Hill's philosophy, I was inspired by the chapter where his son was born without ears and he taught him to hear. Just as Dr. Hill wouldn't give up on his son, I didn't give up on Donna. Every morning on my way down to help take care of Donna, I played the audio tape of *Think and Grow Rich* and stayed the course. I believed if Dr. Hill and his son could be successful, so could Donna and I. I took an unorthodox approach to her recovery that resulted in successful results—in fact, that approach is now a guideline for returning servicemen with brain injuries.

I wrote the book *One More Sunset* for Donna to know the story and for her to know how she was loved and cared for. Now the book is in 60 military hospitals to help the families not give up hope and to know there is a recovery process. It takes time, patience, love, support, and burning desire. Today, Donna is healthy, lives independently, and leads a very full life. Without the philosophy of Napoleon Hill, none of this would have happened.

—JIM CONNELLY

Donna's Italian Beef with Manicotti

- 3 pounds boneless rump or chuck roast
- 1/2 cup Italian bread crumbs
- 1/2 cup parmesan cheese
- 1 teaspoon dry mustard
- 1/2 teaspoon oregano
- 1/4 teaspoon salt
- 1/4 teaspoon coarse black pepper
- 4 tablespoons olive oil
- 3 cloves garlic, finely minced
- 1 onion, thinly sliced
- 1 can (14 ounces) diced Italian tomatoes
- 1 jar (16 ounces) pasta sauce
- 1 package (16 ounces) manicotti noodles

Preheat oven to 375 degrees.

Rinse roast and pat dry.

Mix bread crumbs, parmesan cheese, dry mustard, oregano and salt and pepper in a big bowl.

Rub roast with a little olive oil then coat with bread crumb mixture.

In large heavy skillet, sauté garlic and onion in olive oil until soft. Add roast and quickly brown on all sides.

Transfer meat along with garlic and onions to a roasting pan. Pour can of tomatoes and pasta sauce over roast and bake covered for about 1 1/2 hours.

Remove from oven and let stand.

Prepare manicotti according to instructions. Slice beef, place on dish and spoon tomato sauce over meat. Serve over pasta.

I grew up in the projects of a small factory town in western Pennsylvania. Struggle and survival were life's lessons and I was determined to be a winner. Napoleon Hill came into my life when I was in my twenties and he has been my role model and my inspiration ever since. I now am an entrepreneur and mentor, helping people with life skills, health, and wealth.

Recipe Notes:

"Watch the one ahead of you, and you'll learn why he is ahead. Then emulate him."

2. Mastermind Alliance

Mastermind Alliance is two or more minds working together in perfect harmony for the attainment of a common objective. The process might be likened to either of the two recipes below. Individually, none of the ingredients in either the soup or the dessert recipe is outstanding, but combined together they create a wonderful melody of flavors that can be compared to the workings of a **Mastermind Alliance**. Alone a member may not be able to accomplish much, but combined with the total membership the group power becomes unstoppable. There is power in unity and in the blending of ingredients and spices. Try it for yourself.
- Judith Williamson

Chicken Tortilla Soup

½ c. onion, chopped
1 tsp. fresh garlic minced
2 T. butter or margarine
3-10½ oz. cans chicken broth
1-16 oz. jar picante sauce
2 c. chicken breasts, cooked and shredded
½ c. red bell pepper chopped
¼ tsp. coarsely ground black pepper
2 bay leaves
½ c. vegetable oil
6 corn tortillas, cut into ½-inch strips.
2 avocados, peeled and cut into ½-inch pieces
1 c. cheddar cheese, shredded
sour cream
jalapeño peppers, chopped
cilantro for garnish

In Dutch oven, cook onion and garlic in butter over medium heat, stirring occasionally, until onion is tender. Add chicken broth, picante sauce, shredded chicken, bell pepper, pepper and bay leaves. Bring to a boil. Cover, reduce heat to low. Simmer, stirring occasionally, 20 minutes. Remove bay leaves. In large skillet, heat oil over medium heat until hot. Fry tortilla strips in oil until light golden brown. Drain. Divide tortilla strips among 6 serving bowls; ladle soup over strips. Top with avocado, shredded cheese, sour cream, and jalapeño pepper and cilantro, if desired.

Note: Soup tastes very authentic and is a quick to fix light dinner entrée.

Heavenly Fluff

2 boxes orange jello
1 small can frozen orange juice
2 small cans Mandarin oranges
¾ c. milk
1 (1 lb. can) crushed pineapple
1 (3 oz.) pkg. lemon instant pudding
1 small container of cool whip

Combine orange jello with 1 cup boiling water. Add frozen orange juice, Mandarin oranges (drained) and crushed pineapple (not drained). Mix well and refrigerate until congealed.

Topping: To lemon pudding mix, add ¾ very cold milk and whip until thick in a chilled bowl. Combine pudding mixture and cool whip and spread on top of prepared jello. Chill and serve.

Note: An elegant and easy addition to any buffet.

Mastermind Alliance

> "...two or more minds working together in perfect harmony for the attainment of a common objective."
>
> -Napoleon Hill

Recipe for Success Compact with Invisible Princes

This Mastermind Alliance Recognizes: _____

To Whom Napoleon Hill grants the privilege of being served by his personal guides who operate on the higher levels of intelligence, the names and the services to be rendered by each being as follows:

Prince of Hope

To keep the future enriched with the promise of success and abundance.

Prince of Faith

To provide direct contact with infinite intelligence.

Prince of Love

To keep both body and mind youthful regardless of the passing years.

Prince of Sound Health

To keep the physical body healed and efficient at all times.

Prince of Prosperity

To provide all the money and opportunity for success that is needed.

Prince of Peace of Mind

To keep the mind free from all forms of fear and causes of worry.

Prince of Romance

To give joy and enthusiasm to every thought and every deed.

Prince of Patience

To provide self-discipline sufficient to meet all circumstances with a positive mental attitude.

Prince of Over-All Wisdom

To keep the other eight Princes eternally active in behalf of the makers of this compact.

I hereby gratefully accept the services of the nine invisible Princes and promise to express my gratitude to them each day.

Countersigned by: _____ Signed: _____

Recipe for a Master Mind Compact with Yourself

1. Relate yourself to the nine invisible guides precisely as if they were real people in the flesh, and talk to them in the same friendly tone of voice as you would talk to personal friends.

2. Express your gratitude to the guides at the close of each day, just before retiring, <u>thanking each one individually</u> for the service you have received today, the service that the Guide will render you while you sleep, and the service that will be rendered you tomorrow.

3. Before beginning any plan or the pursuit of any aim or purpose ask the Guides to condition your mind for successful termination of your activity, and <u>thank them in advance</u> for having blessed you with success.

4. When you are in doubt regarding any plan or purpose you may have in mind, before reaching a decision request the guide of Over-all Wisdom to give you directions.

5. Before engaging in any sort of negotiation with other people in connection with your occupation, business or profession, request your Guides to condition the minds of those with whom you contemplate such relationship so they will be favorable to you. (If you are engaged in any form of selling, this habit, if sincerely adhered to, will work miracles for you.)

6. BELIEVE that all requests you make of your Guides will be granted, that all services you request of them will be rendered. (But be careful not to request of them any form of service which would injure another person, or cause another person a loss of any nature whatsoever.)

7. The Guiding Princes work only for gratitude, therefore express your gratitude to them <u>both before and after they serve you</u>.

8. This Master-Mind Compact gives you the privilege of tuning in on the success beam of Napoleon Hill, therefore end all of your requests for services by the Guides by an expression of gratitude for this privilege.

9. The results you will experience from the Master Mind alliance with Napoleon Hill will become noticeable in exact proportion to your development of FAITH in its efficacy.

10. The principle upon which the Master-Mind Compact is based is scientifically sound and it does not interfere, in any manner whatsoever, with anyone's religious beliefs, since the essence of it is based on FAITH, and the power of FAITH is an accepted essential of all religions.

Napoleon Hill

Hang In There! Some Things Just Take Time

My family would gladly confirm that ever since I was a young adult, I have wanted to put together a "spiritual" magazine to help other people feel better. I just didn't know how to get started. My vision remained just that, but on and off through the years I thought about it.

About twenty years ago, I started working for a craft publishing company, but it wasn't until two years ago, when two colleagues and I, without being aware of Napoleon Hill's work, formed what actually was a Mastermind Alliance: an alliance of two or more minds working together in perfect harmony for the attainment of a definite objective. The three of us all seemed to have the same vision for a magazine, and through cooperative effort and harmony put together a presentation for our publisher. It was accepted, and *Pure Inspiration* magazine was born. Looking back, it's interesting to see how it took the alliance of three like-minded individuals to finally bring what had been my initial vision (and theirs) to reality.

And now it is taking Applied Faith to keep it going. The three of us believe that working on this magazine is all about achieving our definite purpose in life. We want to help others and through the magazine, by emphasizing humanity's similarities rather than our differences, we hope to do just that. *Pure Inspiration* is about positive thinking and uplifting messages and I love working on it. I am eternally grateful for the privilege of doing this work. It is truly a labor of love.

—MARIE ARNOLD

Veggie Lasagna

- 1 package (16 ounces) lasagna noodles
- 4 cups (32 ounces) ricotta cheese
- 1 package (8 ounces) cream cheese, softened
- 3/4 cup milk
- 1/2 cup onion, minced
- 1-1/2 teaspoon basil
- 1 teaspoon garlic powder
- 1/2 teaspoon oregano leaves
- 2 cups broccoli florets
- 1 cup carrots. shredded
- 4 cups (16 ounces) low moisture mozzarella cheese, grated
- 3/4 cup parmesan cheese, grated

Cook noodles and drain. Rinse in cold water. Lay flat on paper towels.

Combine ricotta, cream cheese, milk, onion, basil, garlic powder, and oregano. Blend until smooth.

Add broccoli and carrots and mix.

Spread 3/4 cup of vegetable mixture on the bottom of a 13-inch by 9-inch baking dish.

Add one layer of noodles on top, then 1/4 of remaining vegetable mix. Sprinkle with mozzarella and parmesan.

Repeat layers, ending with cheese.

Bake at 375 degrees for 50 minutes or until hot and bubbly.

Let stand 10 minutes and serve.

If you ever think the answers are too long in coming and you feel like giving up—don't! Have faith in Infinite Intelligence. The unfolding of the universe and our lives is not according to our timing, but His!

Marie Arnold is Managing Editor of *Pure Inspiration* magazine.

The Positive You

The Mastermind Principle—two or more minds working together in the spirit of perfect harmony toward the attainment of a definite major purpose—is one of the most powerful principles of success. I believe this principle begins with us. We are all two people: a positive person and a negative person.

The first time I experienced this principle was in 1967 at the age of 20. I was in Basic Training for the U. S. Army during the height of the Vietnam War. I received orders for assignment to the Advanced Infantry Training Base. I never thought for a second that I would become a combat soldier. I was overwhelmed by negative thoughts. *Why me? What did I do to deserve this? How can I tell my mother that I'm going to Vietnam?* I had never before experienced this feeling of self-pity and fear. I had never before recognized the Negative Me.

As I stood in line waiting to call home, holding back the tears, I had only negative thoughts. But when I heard my mother's voice, I became very calm, and said, "I got my orders for Fort Polk, Louisiana." "What does that mean?" she asked. "It means I am going to get the best training, from the best army, from the best country in the world. And when I come back from Vietnam, I'm going to college on the G. I. Bill." Within 30 minutes' time I had experienced the extreme emotions of the positive and negative me. It wasn't until five years later when I read **Think and Grow Rich** that I learned what happened that day. I learned we are all two people. We must never become the negative person. Whenever I have negative thoughts, I remind myself of that day.

—RAYMOND CAMPBELL

Michigan White Bean Chicken Chili

2 skinless chicken breasts, cut into bite-size pieces
1/2 onion, chopped
1 teaspoon garlic, minced
1 can (16 ounces) chicken broth
1 can (4 ounces) chopped green chiles
1 large jar (48 ounces) Great Northern White Michigan beans
1 teaspoon ground cumin
1/2 teaspoon oregano
2 dashes Tabasco or other hot sauce

In large Dutch oven, brown chicken, onion, and garlic in small amount of broth.

Add chiles in juice, stir and cook for one minute.

Add beans with liquid, remainder of broth, cumin, oregano, and hot sauce.

Stir well and simmer one hour or longer. Chili thickens as it cooks.

Eat with a spoon, or better yet, with tortilla chips.

As a Vietnam veteran I returned from the war seeking a new direction in life. I found it in Napoleon Hill's **Think and Grow Rich.** *With renewed purpose, I graduated from Walsh College and became a CPA. I founded Raymond Campbell & Company, CPAs, the first of several companies I steadily built into successful businesses. I have a 30-year track record of success as an entrepreneur. I am currently President and CEO of Mastermind Solutions Inc. and continue to be an ardent believer and teacher of the Mastermind Principle.*

Establish a Mastermind Alliance

I had determined years ago to own my own business. However, I knew I wanted no employees, the freedom and flexibility to work anywhere I wanted to in the world at any time, and to make money while I slept—not trading hours for dollars. I did not know what type of business it would be and how it would work, but my faith never wavered that I would succeed.

Through the years I worked a job during the day and spent my evenings and weekends on my business ideas. Some things worked. Some didn't. But I kept focused on my goal always. The only thing missing was a mastermind partner.

One day my boss called me into his office to meet a man who had questions about an area I was responsible for. The moment I walked in and met Jim Connelly, I knew I had met someone extraordinary. We clicked immediately.

Two weeks later Jim stopped by my office and I had the opportunity to ask about his success. He mentioned the book *Think and Grow Rich*. Out from under some papers, I pulled my 1954 vintage copy of that book and his eyes got big. From that day on, we've been inseparable business partners and a mastermind team. Never has the future looked so bright.

—Nina Hershberger

Corn Casserole

1 can creamed corn
1 can whole corn (drained)
2 eggs
1 cup sour cream
1 stick butter
1 box Jiffy corn bread mix

Preheat oven to 350 degrees.

Mix all ingredients together.

Pour into 9-inch square baking dish.

Bake for 50 minutes.

Simple and delicious.

My passion in business has been direct response marketing. I have a particular flair for creating unique, money-making direct mail pieces—I'm known as the "wallet mailer lady" because of one of my ideas. I work with businesses of all sizes to increase marketing response through direct mail.

W. Clement Stone cooking with PMA

Recipe Notes

3. Applied Faith

Applied Faith is an active state of mind through which individuals seek to establish a working relationship with Infinite Intelligence. Through applied faith minds are conditioned to receive guidance from Infinite Intelligence in the form of a plan. Dr. Hill states that when the plan comes through to your conscious mind, you are to accept it with appreciation and gratitude – and act on it at once. You will recognize that this is the correct plan by the feeling of intense enthusiasm and inspiration that accompanies its reception. This inspiration and enthusiasm is felt too for the two appetizer recipes below. When the Bacon Wraps are cooking, the entire house smells wonderful. Nobody can wait another minute to sample these delicious tidbits. The Enthusiasm is visible. There is another reason for liking the Stuffed Mushrooms. They can be made to be low in calories and low in cost. This recipe inspires you to be true to your diet since you are satisfying your cravings, but not caving into an enormous amount of calories.

- Judith Williamson

Bacon Wraps

1 lb. bacon slices cut in half

pineapple chunks

water chestnuts (whole)

Mandarin orange slices

maraschino cherries

Wrap ½ bacon slice around pineapple chunks, water chestnuts, Mandarin orange slices and maraschino cherries. Close with toothpicks.

Bake 20 to 30 minutes at 400 degrees until bacon is done.

Drain on paper towels.

Sauce:

¼ cup chili sauce

¼ cup Miracle Whip (not mayo)

½ cup brown sugar

Mix sauce ingredients and pour over the bacon wraps.

Return to a 350 degree oven and bake for 15 to 20 minutes more.

Note: These are irresistible. The smell invites everyone into the kitchen to see what is cooking. There will be no leftovers.

Baked Mushrooms

1 lb. medium mushrooms

1 pkg. cornbread Stove Top stuffing

Parsley, for garnish

Remove mushroom stems and chop. Prepare stuffing according to package directions. Add chopped stems to stuffing. Mix well. Fill caps with a well-rounded portion of the mixture. Arrange mushrooms in a baking pan with sides touching and bake at 350 degrees for 20 to 25 minutes. Garnish with parsley, if desired.

Note: Makes an attractive and tasty, low fat appetizer.

Applied Faith

> *" When a plan comes through to your conscious mind...accept it with appreciation and gratitude and act on it at once. "*
>
> -Napoleon Hill

Recipe for Hope and Promise

This was adapted from a message written by Napoleon Hill at the beginning of 1915 when he was president of the Betsy Ross Candy Shop System in Chicago, more than two decades before he published his classic best-seller, *Think and Grow Rich*.

As one year ends and another begins, and while the Yuletide spirit is yet alive, let us stop for a moment and consider some of the blessings for which we should be thankful. Let us take a personal inventory of our Divine rewards and see whether or not the year, which has moved us a step closer to the great unknown beyond, has helped make us a truly better and further advanced civilization.

I have no right or desire to judge the degree of advancement which others have made, or what blessings they have received, but personally I have much for which I am truly thankful.

FIRST, I have been abundantly blessed with good health and strength of both body and mind.

SECOND, I have two fine young boys and their darling mother who are also blessed with health and strength of body and mind. These dear ones are a constant source of inspiration to me in my efforts to be a successful businessman and a loyal and patriotic American.

THIRD, I possess the undisturbed right to labor freely for these loved ones in my selected vocation in a country that offers an abundance of encouragement and protection to the legitimate producer of human necessities.

FOURTH, I enjoy citizenship in a country that is free from war and its attendant suffering, a country where love for peace, respect for the home, and reverence of God are dominant in the minds of its people.

FIFTH, I enjoy the commercial monument which I have steadily built up with the help of many others and through my own long hours of effort and unceasing determination. I shall not pass into the New Year without seeing my dreams of success realized.

SIXTH, I have no fault to find with anyone on earth. I am at peace with all my fellowmen. I am in a state of mental attitude which leave me free to work effectively and aggressively during the New Year. If I have done any good deeds during the past year, I hope to double them during the next. If I have been useful to any human being during the old year, I hope to be doubly useful during the New Year.

Recipe for Faith

1. Faith is a state of mind which enables one to visualize one's central purpose or one's minor plans and purposes as achieved even before beginning the pursuit.

2. Faith is a state of mind which can be induced through intensity of desire backed by persistent suggestion to the subconscious mind that the object of that desire shall become fully realized and attained.

3. Faith begins to take the place of doubt when one recognizes the existence and availability of infinite intelligence.

4. Faith multiplies itself through use! The more one relies upon it, the more pronounced it becomes.

5. Faith is Nature's elixir through the use of which Nature enables man to transmute the impulse of thought into a sky-scraper of riches or a hovel of poverty.

APPLIED FAITH

Impossible or Incredible?

In October 2005, Judy Williamson and I conceived the idea of an international convention devoted to Dr. Hill's philosophy. I took on the role of organizing the convention, to be held in Malaysia. Little did I know what I was getting into! The convention grew to include a world-premiere event for *Millionaire: Awaken Your Secret* and a convention hall large enough to seat 2,776.

Without Applied Faith, I could never have overcome the fears and doubts I encountered during this project. I had to have faith in myself, in Judy, in everyone who worked with us, and in Infinite Intelligence. I focused my thoughts daily on the success of the convention until March 12, 2007, when the event was opened by Malaysia's Prime Minister, Datuk Seri Ahmad Badawi.

Here is my recipe for developing and employing Applied Faith:

1. Know what you want and believe that you can and will get it.
2. Express gratitude many times daily for having already received what you want.
3. Keep your mind open for hunches, and when you are inspired for action, move at once.
4. When defeat comes, accept it as nothing more than a challenge to keep on trying.
5. Believe in yourself and act, and keep acting.
6. Whenever doubt creeps in, treat it for what it is: just a doubt. Believe your beliefs and doubt your doubts.
7. Start where you are, with what you have, knowing that what you have is plenty enough.

—CHRISTINA CHIA

Szechuan Hot and Sour Soup

- 2 tbsp. vegetable oil
- 1 clove garlic, minced
- 2 cans (28 ounces) chicken stock
- 5 dried shiitake mushrooms, soaked in water till soft, then julienned
- 3 pieces canned bamboo shoots, julienned
- 1 carrot, peeled and julienned
- 4 ounces firm tofu, diced into 1/4-inch cubes
- 1 tablespoon vinegar
- 1 teaspoon soy sauce
- 1/2 teaspoon sugar
- 2 teaspoons white pepper
- 2 tablespoons corn starch
- 1/2 cup cold water
- 1 egg
- 1 sprig of cilantro, chopped

In a 2-quart pot, heat oil and sauté garlic until fragrant. Add chicken stock and bring to a boil.

Add bamboo shoots, carrots, mushrooms, and tofu. Simmer until vegetables are fairly soft (about 10 minutes, depending how finely they are chopped).

Add vinegar, soy sauce, sugar, and pepper.

Stir corn starch in water until completely dissolved. Add to pot. Return to boil to thicken soup, stirring constantly.

Remove from heat.

Crack egg into a cup. Leave whole, do not beat. While stirring the soup vigorously, pour egg in, forming white "threads" as it cooks.

Serve immediately. Garnish with chopped cilantro.

Born in Singapore, the eldest of eight children, my dream was to become a lawyer. At 17, I had to help support the family, and I spent the next 2 years training as a dental nurse. I worked while attending the university for the next three years, but needed more schooling for the law degree. For five years I saved all I could, and at age 25, I began law school in London. To fulfill the requirements of the Malaysian bar took another eight years, but with applied faith and definiteness of purpose, I have built a law firm supporting 40 employees. Napoleon Hill Associates is my other venture, formed to spread Dr. Hill's philosophy in southeast Asia and Australia.

Awaken Your Secret

One moment I had a movie for Julia Roberts and was living in the Hollywood Hills, the next moment Julia fell out of love and didn't want to make a romantic comedy! I spiraled into debt, to the tune of over a hundred thousand dollars. My faith was broken and my spirit was in shreds, as my fiancée left me.

My Achilles' heel as I turned 40 years old was money. This incredible resource was obviously beyond me, indicated by this small fact: whenever I passed cash laying on the street, I'd say, "It's only a penny."

As I sat penniless in my brother's empty apartment back in London, I prayed for divine grace. It was at that moment a friend gave me Napoleon Hill's *Think and Grow Rich*. As I read each chapter, my mind raced. "What if I turn my only possession, a camera, onto myself and see if Napoleon Hill's Success Principles hold true with millionaires and billionaires today? Can I make a million dollars from creating a movie?"

Over three years later: I have traveled across America five times, filmed on four continents, and had the honor of a world premiere at the Napoleon Hill International Convention in Malaysia, attended by the Prime Minister, with whom I shared the platform.

Napoleon Hill gave me strength and wisdom—now almost a prayer: "I trust Cosmic Habitforce to deliver, with impeccable timing, everything I desire with the highest good for all." As I read Dr. Hill's final book, *Grow Rich With Peace of Mind*, I know that when my last day on Earth has arrived, that I will have lived life like a prayer in action.

—MARTIN DUNKERTON

Chicken With Many Cloves of Garlic

A dish to share with family and friends, enough for six people gathered round the table.

- 1 organic chicken, 4-5 pounds
- 2 tablespoons salt
- 2 tablespoons black pepper
- 40 garlic cloves, unpeeled
- 1 lemon
- 4 sprigs thyme
- 3 ounces (1/2 cup) olive oil
- 2 carrots
- 2 sticks of celery
- 2 shallots
- 2 bay leaves
- 8 ounces apple juice or cider

Preheat oven to 350 degrees.

Prepare chicken by rubbing the skin all over with freshly ground salt and pepper. Put 5 cloves of garlic, lemon, and thyme in the cavity of the chicken.

In a pot with a lid, just big enough to take the chicken, add oil and 10 garlic cloves.

Roughly chop carrots, celery and shallots, and add to the pot. Add the bay leaves.

Put the chicken in the pot, pour over the apple juice or cider, and scatter the remaining garlic over the chicken.

Cover the pot with two layers of cooking foil and the lid. Bake for 1 hour and 15 minutes.

Rest for 10 minutes before bringing to the table. Lift the lid in front of your guests for everyone to catch the wonderful aromas. Serve with fluffy mashed potatoes and a leafy salad.

I have been blessed to have an extraordinary career as an award-winning, Royal Television Society-nominated BBC director. My movie documentary, Millionaire: Awaken Your Secret, *has been nominated for Best International Documentary at the Everglades Film Festival in South Africa. The movie is about to go out into the world and will help millions of people with prosperity. Did I make a million dollars? You'll have to watch the movie!*

APPLIED FAITH

Progress Through Faith

I was introduced to Napoleon Hill's 17 Principles of Success in the spring of 2005. In **Think and Grow Rich**, Dr. Hill says that the secret of his philosophy is there "for all who are ready to receive it." I feel I have not opened up enough to be ready to receive my successes, but I will. I keep practicing the 17 principle as best I can while learning from the insights of others. Napoleon Hill and I will have a prosperous learning relationship for years to come.

Faith needs a foundation on which to stand. Fear exists without a base. As I struggle with my fears by learning to lean more on my faith, I take the baby steps to gradually become what I was meant to be. We know the subconscious mind will translate into reality a thought driven by fear just as readily as it will translate into reality a thought driven by courage, or faith. My faith over my fear is what I am practicing. Fear is still a bigger part of me, but I am willing to risk the fear of failure in order to succeed.

Each of us reaches our potential in our own time. We are taught to always compare ourselves to others when really we should just look in the mirror at ourselves. I choose to keep the positive around me in the knowledge and understanding I seek. I choose to continue to associate with those individuals who enrich me and believe in me. In taking these steps, each individual becomes a true blessing in my life.

—REBECCA JARVIS

Amish Friendship Bread Starter

Make something special to share with a friend! This delicious starter can make a variety of breads. Do not use metal containers or utensils. This starter takes 10 days to finish.

- 1 package (1/4 ounce) active dry yeast
- 1/4 cup warm water (110 degrees)
- 3 cups all-purpose flour
- 3 cups white sugar
- 3 cups milk

In a small bowl, dissolve yeast in water. Let stand 10 minutes.

In a 2-quart glass, plastic, or ceramic container, combine 1 cup flour and 1 cup sugar. Mix thoroughly or flour will lump when milk is added.

Slowly stir in 1 cup milk and dissolved yeast mixture. Cover loosely and let stand until bubbly. Leave loosely covered at room temperature. Consider this day 1 of the 10-day cycle.

On days 2 through 4, stir the starter with a spoon.

On day 5, stir in 1 cup flour, 1 cup sugar, and 1 cup milk.

On days 6 through 9, stir only.

On day 10, stir in 1 cup flour, 1 cup sugar, and 1 cup milk.

Keep 1 cup to make your first bread and give 2 cups to friends, along with this recipe and your favorite Amish Bread recipe. Store the remaining 1 cup of starter in a container in the refrigerator, or begin the 10-day process again (with this starter used as day 1). The starter may also be frozen.

I have witnessed the successes of others, yet feel I have not found my own. I am writing this article for others to know that they are not alone. Even though I feel I have not achieved my potential, I am getting closer, and I will never quit. I enjoy hearing other people's stories while rejoicing with them in their successes. I have faith that as I conceive and believe, I too will achieve. I am pleased to share my testimony with you, for this book is for all of us seeking our secret treasures of life.

Applied Faith Will Get You Through

In recent years, living the emotional roller coaster of being middle aged, seeing children in their last years of college, and contemplating empty nest syndrome, I have really felt a burning desire towards Applied Faith. Napoleon Hill talks about faith as a state of mind that might properly be called the "mainspring of the soul." He also says, "Faith commands the best room in your mind and will not associate with negative thoughts."

Faith requires establishing a working association with Infinite Intelligence (my God in my case), self-discipline, a positive mental attitude, and action. Applied faith will give you spiritual strength to meet any situation, but passive faith benefits no one. Therefore, when you feel moved to do something through the guidance of Infinite Intelligence, you should act on it and not question it. As the Bible states, "But wilt thou know, O vain man, that faith without works is dead?" (James 2:20)

I went by a sign today that made a strong impression on me. It said, "Faith is a Journey, Not a Destination." How could such a simple statement move me so? Think about it. Faith is a journey. You will surely hit some bumps in the road, there may be sharp turns, sometimes you may even get lost. You may have a few detours, you may reach crossroads where you have to choose which way to turn (toward faith or toward fear), and some days you just don't know what is around the corner. Only by relying on faith and experiencing faith's journey can you feel closer to the source of your faith.

—MARYANN WILLIAMSON JONES

Italian Beef

- 4 pounds bottom round beef roast
- 1/2 teaspoon pepper
- 1 tablespoon Italian seasoning
- 1 jar (10 ounces) pepperoncini peppers, with juice
- 4-6 garlic cloves, peeled
- 1 can (16 ounces) beef broth
- 6 beef bouillon cubes

Cut slits in roast and insert garlic cloves.

Add all ingredients to a slow cooker.

Braise on low setting for 8 to 10 hours, or on high for 4 to 5 hours.

Meat can be sliced or shredded with a fork. Serve on hard rolls with additional pepperoncini peppers and mozzarella cheese.

I was blessed to be born in the United States to parents who had strong faith and applied it to their daily lives. My story isn't extraordinary, but I can assure you that no matter who you are, no matter what life your Maker has laid out for you, no matter how many challenges you may face, you can and will benefit from Applied Faith. Applying my faith has made me the person I am today and will change the person I am tomorrow.

APPLIED FAITH

Summon Applied Faith

My family frequently requested Waikiki Chicken for dinner. We savored the sweet and sour tangy flavor of the sauce while talking, laughing, joking, and sharing stories of the day. But in the blink of an eye, life changed: in 2002, our youngest son, Matthew, age 21, was killed in an Army training accident. Losing a child is a parent's worst nightmare, but through the comfort and prayers of our church, minister, friends, and family, we held onto our faith. In measured, painful steps, our faith in God and His promises gave us the ability to cope with this terrible loss.

In 2006, my husband of 38 years died very unexpectedly. Larry was only 58. It is awful to lose a child, but worse is to lose a partner. When your child dies, part of you also goes to the grave, but when you lose a husband or wife, you lose part of your own identity. Four months later my mother passed away. Life seemed to spiral into a deep chasm, yet somewhere in the darkness was the light of my faith and belief that even when God's love seemed far away, it was actually there all the time supporting me to fight and carry on. Faith gave me strength to emerge from the darkness and find a new purpose and path in life. Faith has empowered my life toward a kinship and empathy toward others I had not felt before. It has made me aware of how precious life is and to never take for granted that tomorrow is a given, because it is not.

Savor your family this day, tell them how much you love them, and, best of all, keep your faith in working order through prayers and commitment to the greatest of all gifts: love.

—Dee Naifeh

Waikiki Chicken

2 whole chicken legs
2 whole chicken breasts
1/2 cup flour
1/3 cup vegetable oil
1 teaspoon salt
1/4 teaspoon pepper
1 large can (20 ounces) sliced pineapple
1 cup sugar
2 tablespoons corn starch
3/4 cup cider vinegar
1 tablespoon soy sauce
1 chicken bouillon cube
1 large green pepper, cut crosswise in 1/4-inch circles

Preheat oven to 350 degrees.

Wash chicken and pat dry with paper towels.

Coat chicken with flour.

Heat oil in large skillet and add chicken a few pieces at a time. Brown on all sides. Remove and arrange in shallow roasting pan, arranging pieces skin side up. Sprinkle with salt and pepper.

Drain pineapple, pouring syrup into a 2-cup measure. Add water to make 1-1/4 cups liquid.

In medium saucepan, combine pineapple syrup, sugar, corn starch, vinegar, soy sauce and bouillon cube.

Bring to boil, stirring constantly. Boil 2 minutes, then pour over chicken.

Bake, uncovered, 30 minutes.

Add pineapple slices and green pepper; bake 30 minutes longer or until chicken is tender.

Serve with fluffy white rice.

For the past ten years I've been a substitute elementary teacher, often teaching long-term while a teacher is out with illness or pregnancy. When I'm not subbing, I am a frequent flyer to Germany, to visit my oldest son Michael, his wife Viktoria, and their children, Alexander, Kysenia, Matthew, and another on the way in November. Reinventing myself since the deaths of my son, husband, and mother has become a daily process. I'm often surprised at what occurs each day. Maybe it's a phone call from a friend, or enjoying a great cup of coffee, or helping a child; whatever it is, I feel blessed with life's daily beauty, no matter how small or great.

When You Dream and Believe, You Will Achieve

It was the lowest point of my life. I was in the process of losing my business, I had lost complete faith in myself, and to top it off, I was losing my grandmother to cancer. A couple of nights prior to her passing, all the grandchildren were lying on her bed with her, listening to my grandfather tell stories of their youth. My wife also sat with me.

As the night went on, I found myself asking Nonna if she would come and visit when she passed. Her reply was a definite no: "The dead don't visit the living." "What about in my dreams?" I asked. Her reply was the same: "The dead don't visit the living." "What about as a butterfly?" shouted my wife, and my grandmother replied, "Yes, as a butterfly I will!" Not long after, my grandmother passed.

Ten days later, on New Year's Day, my wife and I were walking along a beautiful pathway filled with glorious plants and flowers. I said quietly, "Nonna, you've been gone for ten days and you still haven't visited me. Look how beautiful these colors are, look at the flowers." I did not even get to finish my sentence when the largest, most beautiful butterfly I had ever seen came and flew a figure-eight between my wife and me. As I was telling my wife what I had just said, the butterfly returned and danced for us. It found its way to a twig and flapped its little wings, trying hard just to stay there a moment or two longer. And then off it went.

That was January 1, 2000, and whenever I see a butterfly, I remember my grandmother, and I know that whatever I dare to dream, as long as I believe it, I will achieve it. You never walk alone.

—Emiliano Vitale

Nonna's Spaghetti Napolitana

- 4 tablespoons extra virgin olive oil
- 1 small onion, chopped very fine
- 1 clove garlic, minced
- 1 jar (16 ounces) Passata Fresh Italian Tomato Sauce
- 4 basil leaves (fresh) or 1/2 teaspoon dried
- 2 small hot red chilis, chopped very fine
- 1 teaspoon pesto
- 1 pinch salt
- 1 pinch pepper
- 8 ounces spaghetti
- Parmesan cheese

Heat olive oil in pan. Add onion and sauté until golden.

Add garlic. Continue to sauté until garlic just begins turn golden.

Add jar of sauce. (Substitute your favorite sauce if Passata is not available.)

Add basil, chilis, pesto, salt, and pepper.

Stir thoroughly and reduce heat to simmer.

Cover with lid, leaving a small gap for steam, and cook for 20-25 minutes, stirring every few minutes.

While sauce is cooking, boil pasta per package directions for al dente.

Drain pasta and pour in large serving bowl. Add 3/4 of sauce and mix it thoroughly to coat pasta.

Top with remaining sauce and shave Parmesan on top to taste.

*As a dreamer, I often found myself lost in a world of fantasy, living the successful life in my head, rather than in my real life. I was always a talented stylist, I just didn't have the commitment and dedication that it took to make a success. It wasn't until I failed in my first business, due to a lack of Definite Major Purpose, that I finally decided to take my life seriously. Then I borrowed **Think and Grow Rich** and realized that I had developed a burning desire for the secret ingredient to my successful life. Through Applied Faith, I followed my instincts and found my way to the principles that inevitably would change my life.*

APPLIED FAITH

Applied Faith and Teamwork Lead to Success

I was introduced to the Napoleon Hill philosophy at a very difficult time in my life. I was widowed at age 55, had been out of the work force for 15 years, and found myself facing insurmountable odds. I had no idea the direction my life would go. I did have great faith and trust in the Lord, but I realized that He helps those who help themselves. I immediately enrolled in computer courses—realizing to get back into any office atmosphere, I had to know something about the computer world. Through the help of a wonderful friend, Phyl Green, I was offered the position as personal secretary to Don Green, President and CEO of Black Diamond Savings Bank. I almost turned the position down, simply because I had been longtime friends with Don and Phyl and I didn't want to impose on their friendship. My family encouraged me to try it, and I am so thankful that I did.

Even though Don's main position was with the bank, he had a great passion for the Napoleon Hill philosophy and the Foundation. He was serving as a trustee at this time and teaching the Science of Success course at our local collage. I immediately became involved with typing his tests, assisting with grading of papers, etc., all the while reading all the material I could get. When Don retired from the bank in 2000, he accepted the position of executive director for the Napoleon Hill Foundation and offered me a part-time position. I accepted while continuing with my full-time position at the bank. From worried and computer illiterate to a personal secretary and assistant for an incredible foundation, my faith led me to great successes.

—ANNEDIA STURGILL

Cheese Ball

2 packages (8 ounces each) cream cheese, softened
1-1/2 cups pecans, chopped
1 can (8 ounces) crushed pineapple, drained
1/4 cup green pepper, chopped
2 tablespoons onion, chopped
1 tablespoon seasoned salt

Beat cream cheese until creamy.

Add 1 cup pecans and remaining ingredients. Mix well.

Chill. When firming up, form into ball and roll in remaining pecans.

Refrigerate at least 1 hour to completely set.

Serve with crackers or cut vegetables.

In 2003, I became a full-time employee of the Napoleon Hill Foundation. I am very proud to be associated with this wonderful organization. I don't have a favorite principle because I think it takes them all, but I know that I came out of adversity, I operate in a positive mental attitude, I practice personal initiative, I go the extra mile, I have been told I have a pleasing personality, and I love being part of the Napoleon Hill team! It takes all of us to fulfill our mission of "making this world a better place in which to live."

Recipe Notes

4. Going the Extra Mile

It is not a time to experiment with new recipes that may not measure up to your expectations when the holidays are upon you and time is short. Here are two easy to make and always successful cookie recipes that never fail to get rave reviews. The ingredients are not expensive and a slight substitution here and there doesn't produce a failure. When doubled, each recipe makes an ample amount for gift giving. Both were given to me by friends when I admired their results. As with any successful recipe, make use of what works. We don't have to reinvent the wheel each time we want to duplicate a success. The **"Going the Extra Mile"** part comes in when you share your cookies with someone else. Sometimes just acknowledging that you have a little gift for someone brightens both of your days. In this way **"Going the Extra Mile"** becomes a reciprocal process that fosters good rapport. Remember to render more service and better service if you want to get good results.

- Judith Williamson

Snowballs

2/3 c. butter

2/3 c. margarine (I use Imperial)

½ c. brown sugar

3 c. flour

1 tsp. salt

2 tsp. vanilla

½ c. finely chopped nuts (I use walnuts or pecans)

Cream butter and shortening with the brown sugar. Sift flour and salt together and add gradually to creamed mixture. Add vanilla and mix well. Add chopped nuts, blend and shape into 1-inch balls or crescents. Bake at 325 degrees for 25 minutes. Cool slightly for 5 to 10 minutes until the cookies harden and then roll in powdered sugar. When completely cool, roll again in powdered sugar.

Note: These are simple to make and the ingredients are not costly. Recipe doubles well.

Homestead Spice Cookies

1 egg

1 cup sugar

¾ c. shortening (I use Imperial)

¼ c. molasses

Cream the above ingredients together.

2 tsp. baking soda

1 tsp. ginger

1 tsp. cinnamon

½ tsp. nutmeg

¼ tsp. cardamom

2 c. flour

Sift the above ingredients together and add to the creamed mixture. Put dough in refrigerator for 8 hours or overnight. Then take a teaspoon full of dough and roll in sugar and place on cookie sheet. Bake in 350 degree oven for 10 minutes.

Note: These cookies smell wonderful when baking. Make sure you chill the dough before baking as directed. When making these cookies, I had no molasses on hand, but I had Bead Molasses used in Chinese cooking. I experimented with the same amount and it worked just fine. Also, I was unable to find the cardamom spice at the grocery store, so I omitted it from the recipe.

Going The Extra Mile

> " *...is the action of rendering more and better service than that for which you are presently paid.* "
>
> -Napoleon Hill

Recipe for the Habit of Doing More

1. This habit turns the spotlight of favorable attention upon those who develop it.

2. This habit enables one to profit by the law of contrast, since the majority of people have formed and apply the opposing habit, by rendering as little service as they can.

3. This habit gives one the benefit of the law of Increasing Returns and insures one against the disadvantages of the law of Decreasing Returns, thus eventually enabling one to receive more pay than one would receive without this habit.

4. This habit insures one preferred employment at preferred wages and permanency of employment as long as there is employment to be had. The person who practices this habit is the last to be removed from the pay-roll when business is poor and the first to be taken back after a lay-off.

5. This habit develops greater skill, efficiency, and also greater earning ability and tends to give one preference over others.

6. This habit makes one practically indispensable to one's employer because it is a habit not found in the majority of people, and because it induces employers to relegate greater responsibilities to those who practice it. The capacity to assume responsibility is the quality which brings the highest monetary returns.

7. This habit leads to promotion because it indicates that those who practice it have ability for supervision and leadership not found in those who follow the opposite habit.

8. This habit enables one to set one's own salary. If it cannot be obtained from one employer, it may be obtained from his competitor.

Recipe for Attracting Attention by Going the Extra Mile

The Habit Of Doing More Than Paid For

1. Just as an arm or a limb of the body grows strong in exact proportion to its use, so does the mind grow strong through use. By rendering the greatest possible amount of service the faculties through which the service is rendered are put into use and, eventually, become strong and accurate.

2. By rendering more service than that for which you are paid, you will be turning the spotlight of favorable attention upon yourself, and it will not be long before you will be sought with fancy offers for your services, and there will be a continuous market for those services.

By rendering more service and better service than that for which you are paid, you thereby take advantage of the Law of Increasing Returns through the operation of which you will eventually be paid, in one way or another, for far more service than you actually perform. Adopt the habit as a part of your life's philosophy, and let it become known by all who know you that you render such service out of choice, not as a matter of accident, but by deliberate intent, and soon you will see keen competition for your service. If I as the author of this philosophy had to choose one of the Seventeen Laws of Success as being the most important, and had to discard all the others except the one chosen, I would, without a moment's hesitation, choose this Law of Rendering More Service and Better Service than paid for.

Your Number One Competitive Advantage

Businesses provide goods and services to their clients. And so do your competitors! Unless you have either a new technology that no competitor has yet developed or a monopoly on the provision of a certain product or service, you will have to maintain a competitive advantage over "the other guy!" The greatest competitive advantage any business has over the competition is going the extra mile.

As a CPA living and working in Israel, it became apparent when I began to develop my accounting practice that what clients most desired was care and attention to their individual needs.

In my accounting practice, going the extra mile was sometimes something as simple as personally calling a client on the phone to remind them that filing deadlines were approaching, or driving to their homes to deliver tax returns when it would have been very inconvenient for them to come to my office. Other times, going the extra mile meant staying up all night working on a report the client had to have the next morning, even though I only received the source documents the night before!

People need to feel they are important. Going the extra mile for your clients or your boss is the best way to let them know they are important to you and that you'll make extra efforts on their behalf.

As Dr. Hill pointed out, most people aren't willing to go the first mile, let alone the extra mile. Incorporating the philosophy of going the extra mile into your work ethic is one of the best ways to ensure that you will come out on top in even the most competitive business or work environments.

—Eliezer A. Alperstein

Sweet Whole Wheat Challah

- 2 cups warm water
- 3 tablespoons dry yeast
- 3/4 cup brown sugar or 1/2 cup of honey
- 2 pounds 70 percent whole wheat flour
- 2 eggs
- 1/2 cup canola oil
- 1 tablespoon salt

Stir in the yeast into 1 cup warm water and add 1 tablespoon brown sugar or honey.

Mix remaining sugar or honey, flour, eggs, and oil in a bowl. When the yeast mixture bubbles, add it to the flour mixture and mix well, gradually adding water from the second cup as needed.

Once the ingredients are incorporated, begin kneading the dough.

While kneading, add the salt, but only after the yeast mixture has been thoroughly mixed in.

Once the dough is a soft but firm ball, put a drop of oil in the bottom of the bowl, just enough to grease it, and allow the dough to rise until it doubles in size. Then punch down the dough and let it rise again for about an hour.

Split the dough into three pieces and roll each into a long cord. Then braid the cords together and make the loaf. Allow dough to rise again for 30–60 minutes.

Bake the loaf at 350 degrees until golden brown.

I was born in 1957 and grew up in Reading, Pennsylvania, northwest of Philadelphia. At the ripe old age of 32, I decided to move to Israel, 6 months before the first Gulf War and the Iraqi missile attacks directed against my newly adopted country. Coming to Israel meant leaving all that was familiar behind, learning a new language, sitting for licensing examinations for my Israeli CPA license, and living through numerous wars and waves of terror. These challenges have made me stronger and have brought out the best in me. I look forward to the future. The best is yet to come.

A Recipe as Simple as QQS

I am happy to inform you, Dr. Hill, that I have kept my promise to you. Yes, it was exactly ten years ago, one Sunday in September 1997, that I "met" you at one of the biggest book stores in Tokyo. Your book title, **Think and Grow Rich**, caught my eye. I was 28 years old and already a successful tour guide of a renowned Japanese tour company. I joined with them on graduation from college because I loved traveling myself. Although I traveled around the world, guiding my clients, my soul was never completely content.

That Sunday, my meeting with you showed me a path to the realization of myself. I was never a big reader, but when I opened **Think and Grow Rich**, I couldn't stop turning the pages. The need for definiteness of purpose was exactly what I had kept feeling in my heart. I realized then that I was destined to succeed, Dr. Hill. My desire to be independent was ignited. My burning desire was clear: I would open a success school based on your philosophy and guide students to their paths for success.

I quit the tour company at the age of 31 and joined a company teaching success philosophy. In that process, I got acquainted with the Napoleon Hill Foundation. Director Judy Williamson helped me pursue the study on the 17 principles of success. In September 2007, just ten years after my path crossed yours, Dr. Hill, my dream came true. I have succeeded in setting up my own success company to motivate people to set goals and achieve them. I have kept and will keep in my mind your "QQS" formula—quality of service, plus quantity of service, done in the proper spirit equals success. With this recipe in hand, anything is possible for me.

—TATSUYA AMINAKA

I consider myself a "motivational educator," teaching my students how to set and achieve goals. I am currently president of Human Unity LLC, an organization for human resources development and management. I am a certified instructor of the Napoleon Hill Foundation, a certified professional coactive coach from CTI, and an NLP Master Practitioner.

Aminaka's Sukiyaki

(4 servings)

2 pounds of very thinly sliced beef

1 roasted bean curd (to be cut in 8 pieces)

2 small onions (to be cut into 12 slices)

1 long green onion (white stem is to be used mainly and cut obliquely into 10 pieces)

4 mushrooms (called shiitake mushroom in Japan; stems to be removed)

1/2 bag of dried gluten (to be soaked in water and then water should be squeezed out)

1 cup of water with dried kelp in it (dried kelp is to be soaked in water at least for 1/2 hour)

Ignite the gas of the portable burner on the table

Heat sukiyaki-pan (about 1 and 1/2 inch-deep pan) with beef lard in it.

Put half of the thinly sliced beef in the pan.

When beef starts to cook, add the following in this order: one cup of sake (Japanese rice wine), two spoonfuls of sugar (depending upon your taste) and 1 cup of soy sauce (depending upon your taste).

Add half of onions, green onions, bean curd, and mushrooms depending upon your taste. Add some water with dried kelp in it.

Add dried gluten.

When cooked, eat immediately and never overcook.

When you finish beef, put the rest of the thinly sliced beef in the pot.

Repeat in the same order, mindful of your favorite seasoning.

Boil, eat immediately, and never overcook to relish sukiyaki.

*Sukiyaki literally means "favorite cooking" in Japanese. You eat very hot cooking in your own or your partner's favorite seasoning.

GOING THE EXTRA MILE

Walk Awhile With Me!

A wise person once said that "to know a man you must first walk a mile in his shoes." How powerful a statement it is to say to another that you are prepared to go an extra mile for them in your own shoes! You do this for them—not for you.

I have been teaching in an all-boys disadvantaged city school in the Republic Of Ireland for the past 12 years. Dr. Hill's philosophy has been a huge part of my students' lives for the past two years. This is all due to the application of the principle of Going the Extra Mile. My first true encounter of this principle at work was during my initial contact with Judy Williamson at the Napoleon Hill World Learning Center. Having explained my circumstances to her and having relayed the stories of my students constantly struggling to find a compass for life, Judy stepped up to the mark and said, "Philip, I will walk this journey with you and together we will show your students the way."

That way is Dr. Hill's way—a path of purpose, determination, and success. I have now completed two years of teaching Napoleon Hill's philosophy to my students and already the transformation in some of their lives is truly astounding! My students all know that through living out the principle of going the extra mile, they have a new set of tools for life—a compass to guide them and a principle to live by. "Do unto others as you would have them do unto you:" If you can't go the extra mile with someone, then go it for them! You always get that mile back in spades. Judy's tiny light of hope has lit fires of purpose and success in souls who otherwise may have been consigned to walk the path of life alone.

—Philip McCauley

Traditional Irish Stew

- 2 pounds rack or shoulder of lamb
- 2 pounds potatoes
- 4 large onions
- 2 leeks, washed and cut into 1-inch rings
- 2 celery stalks, cut into 1/2-inch pieces
- 1 pint cold water or light lamb stock
- 1 tablespoon parsley, chopped
- 1 tablespoon fresh thyme
- 1 small sprig of rosemary
  brown gravy mix
  salt and freshly ground pepper to taste
  fresh parsley, chopped, to garnish

Wipe meat and remove fat and gristle.

Wash and peel potatoes. Cut into quarters.

Remove skin from onion and slice into narrow rings.

Prepare other vegetables by washing and slicing into slices or small chunks.

Bring potatoes and meat to a boil in stock or water and let simmer for 10 minutes. Add the rest of the vegetables.

Tie parsley, thyme, and rosemary together in a bouquet garni and place on top.

Simmer for 30 minutes.

Mix 1 tablespoon of gravy mix with cold water and slowly add to stew. This will thicken and flavor the stock.

Add salt and pepper to taste. Garnish with parsley.

Serve on a plate or large soup dish with knife, fork and spoon. Brown soda bread and salted butter should also be served at the table.

I am a young teacher who was born and raised in Dublin City amongst a family of teachers. I've been teaching in an all-boys disadvantaged secondary school for the past 12 years. The school is in north Dublin, the capital of the Republic of Ireland.

Do You Have That Something Extra?

Going The Extra Mile means the willingness to do something extra of your own free will without being asked. This principle has brought me many successes in many different ways and I am glad to share them with you. The principle of going the extra mile propelled me from a low-grade primary school student in 1976 to a First-Class Honor graduate in Electrical & Electronics Engineering in 1995. This transformation happened after I figured out that I must do something extra in order to outperform my peers. What I did then was simple: I put in extra hours of study and made an effort to read additional books to supplement those already studied in school. If a normal guy like me could achieve academic excellence by going the extra mile, I am sure anyone who practices this principle can achieve great results too.

Going the extra mile will also pave the way for you to get the promotion and monetary rewards you are aiming for. "Extra mile" here means the investment you make in yourself by acquiring new skills and knowledge that are relevant to your job. You should perform this "software upgrade" voluntarily, even if your company does not provide such training. Your additional skill set will differentiate you from your colleagues and you will be the natural choice for promotion when the opportunity arises.

Remember this, opportunities only come to those who are prepared and ready to receive them. To be successful, you must have that something extra that makes you different. By reading this passage now, you are already going the extra mile. If you continue this path, your life will never be the same.

—Tan Juan Keat

Soy Milk

I am not a great cook, so instead of a recipe to prepare, I suggest a drink you may have never tried. Besides coffee and tea, the most popular drink in Singapore is soy milk.

Personally, I will drink a cup of either warm or cold soy milk in the morning after I wake up. Soy milk is made from soy beans, and since it looks milky, we call it soy milk.

Soy bean is cultivated exclusively in south Asian countries and the United States. Products made from soy bean are very popular in Singapore, China, Taiwan, Japan, and Korea. In Singapore, sugar is added to soy milk to sweeten it, and we normally take it with our breakfast. In Taiwan, they have the famous "smelly" tofu which you can detect from quite a distance away. In Japan, soy is a key ingredient in the famous miso soup; there is also a spicy tofu soup in Korea.

One thing to note is that soy bean contains very high protein and should be avoided for people with kidney diseases.

A cup of chilled cold soy milk is the perfect answer to the hot and humid weather in Singapore. Do remember to drink a cup of soy milk when you visit Singapore!

I am from Singapore, a tiny but cosmopolitan city-state located near the equator at the heart of southeast Asia. Our leaders' vision for Singapore is to develop it into a prosperous country based on justice and equality regardless of race, language, or religion. However, an inspiring vision without action is like building a castle in the air. Our leaders execute their vision by going the extra mile, a positive trait for us to learn from. Singapore was built from scrap, with no natural resources, no army, no jobs, and no water to start with. Going the extra mile can help you achieve your personal success the way we did in Singapore.

Better to Give Than Receive

All my life I have done what ever it took to help people in any way that my God-given talents would allow me to do. Whether it was helping students be as successful in my classroom as they possibly could, or helping my children develop into honest, loving, and independent individuals, my life has been devoted to being a caring and sharing spouse and lending a helping hand to my friends or whomever I could. Going the extra mile helped me achieve the best I could be.

—ROSE WRIGHT

"Happiness may be had only by helping others to find it."

"The one and only thing any man has to give in return for the material riches he desires is useful service."

"The greatest of all gifts is the gift of an opportunity for one to help himself."

-NAPOLEON HILL

Delicious Grape Salad

2 pounds seedless red grapes
3 ounces cream cheese
1/2 cup sour cream
1 cup pecan pieces
1 teaspoon vanilla
1 teaspoon sugar, to taste
brown sugar, for garnish

Mix all ingredients together, adding just enough sugar to your liking.

Top with a sprinkle of brown sugar and serve.

I was raised by parents who believed in doing for others and educating girls, therefore the path my life has taken is not surprising. I hold a Bachelors and Masters Degree in Home Economics with an emphasis on curriculum and supervision. I taught high school 28 years while serving as department chairperson in a large integrated high school system in the south suburban suburbs of Chicago. This choice of career permitted me to use my education and talents enriching the lives of many students. I was blessed with a talented, interesting, loving husband and two challenging, capable sons who have contributed to the enrichment of my life.

A Sweet Recipe for Sweet Success

My greatest aim in life is to use each day to serve others in excellence by going the extra mile. I have been in the field of optometry for the past 14 years, working along with my husband, Steven. As the director and a vision therapist for Levin Eye Care Center in Whiting, Indiana, I use Napoleon Hill's 17 principles daily to serve those I have been privileged to care for. Our entire staff has learned Dr. Hill's principles and they apply them both at work and in their personal life.

Before learning about Dr. Hill through Judy Williamson, I learned the value of hard work and diligence from both my parents and grandparents. My grandparents lived on a farm in Flint, Michigan, where they raised pigs, cattle, and chickens, tended strawberry patches, and grew watermelons. I would visit them during my summer months. These were my best vacations, being with family.

I learned from my grandmother how to always make the most of my time and to apply myself during the whole day. When visiting her on the farm, I saw how she was always productive—not busy, but producing much with her time. Farmers are a wonderful example of individuals who apply themselves at the crack of dawn, when the rooster crows, and retiring when the sun sets. One of the reasons is because they have to work with nature, where standards and principles are set in divine order. The other reason is simply because of the love and joy of what nature has to offer each day. Mother Nature always goes the extra mile, producing more than is needed, and I believe we should follow that example in our lives.

—LORETTA LEVIN

Migas

- 4 large eggs
- 2 6-inch round corn tortillas, torn into small pieces
- 1/4 cup milk
- 2 tablespoons olive oil
- 1 large red tomato, seeded, pulped, drained, and diced
- 2 teaspoons fresh cilantro
- 1/4 cup white onion, diced
- 1/8 teaspoon salt
- 1/8 teaspoon pepper
- 1 jalapeño, finely minced, or 1/2 cup sautéed bell pepper (optional)

In a small bowl, mix eggs and milk together until fluffy. Soak tortillas in the egg mixture. Add onion and set aside.

Heat skillet over medium heat. Add olive oil when hot. Then pour egg mixture in. Use a spatula to constantly turn the mixture so eggs will not become overcooked and to keep tortillas fully coated.

Turn the heat down to low and add the diced tomatoes and fresh cilantro. If you want spicy eggs, add bell pepper or jalapeño now. Sprinkle with salt and pepper.

Remove skillet from heat, but continue stirring the mixture to coat the tortillas and keep the eggs moist and fluffy.

Serve immediately. Spoon onto plates and add additional salt and pepper to taste. I recommend a hot cup of coffee if you are serving this dish for breakfast. Savor the warm dish with a warm cup of gourmet coffee and you won't feel like leaving the table. Life is meant to be savored!

For all I have learned in life, I would like to express my appreciation to my family, Dr. Hill, and especially the Napoleon Hill World Learning Center, for expanding my awareness and understanding of going the extra mile. Without the dedication and determination of Dr. Hill, we would not have the necessary tools to be the successful people we are today. We must help others simply out of love and gratitude. The truest form of success is when you are sharing your blessings with another to enrich the quality of life in the world.

Where will you be ten years from now if you keep on going the way you are going?
  - Napoleon Hill

5. Pleasing Personality

A **Pleasing Personality** is the aggregate of all the agreeable, gratifying, and likable qualities of any one individual. It is good to be aware of the thirty traits that contribute to a person's character makeup. It is even better to be aware of the single most important trait which is a positive mental attitude. Without a positive mental attitude, even if you possessed all the other traits, your personality would be of little use to you in your success journey. With a wholesome mental attitude, you can project a positive influence on those around you. This in turn enables you to influence the outcome of your desire.

The Carolina Cole Slaw and Rosy Glow Punch recipes are two pleasing additions to this cookbook. Each presents itself nicely on the table and offers a colorful display. Why not try both of them at your next picnic or BBQ?

— Judith Williamson

Carolina Cole Slaw

1 medium head cabbage, chopped

(Or, two bags of cut up cole slaw mix.)

1 green pepper, chopped

1 red pepper, chopped

1 yellow pepper, chopped

1 onion, chopped

1 c. vinegar

¾ c. sugar

½ c. oil

1 tsp. salt

1 T. celery seed

1 tsp. mustard powder

Mix vinegar, sugar, salt, oil, salt, celery seed, and mustard powder. Boil for a few minutes. Pour over chopped mixed ingredients. Chill.

Note: Will keep in the refrigeration for days.

Rosy Glow Punch

3 bottles (1 quart each) cranberry juice cocktail, chilled

1 can (12 ounces) frozen lemonade concentrate, thawed

½ gallon raspberry sherbet

1 quart ginger ale, chilled

mint sprigs, optional

Combine cranberry cocktail and lemonade concentrate. Stir well, chill. Just before serving pour into 4 quart punch bowl. Add scoops of raspberry sherbet. Slowly add ginger ale. Garnish with mint sprigs.

Makes 50 servings.

Pleasing Personality

> *"...the sum total of one's mental, spiritual, and physical traits and habits that distinguish one from all others."*
> -Napoleon Hill

Recipe to Develop Self-Confidence

1. Start out by taking the first step toward success: Choose a definite major goal in life and concentrate upon it until it becomes a burning desire. You can't win a race until you know where the finish line lies.

2. Having decided what you want to do, the goal you wish to attain, memorize this statement, repeating it until you are convinced of its truth: "Whatever I desire to do, I can do."

3. Don't over-build the importance of decisions in your own mind. Make decisions, both big or small, as rapidly as possible. Remember there are few mistakes that can't be corrected, if necessary.

4. Your lack of confidence is a form of fear. It can be licked in the same way you overcome fear. Bring it out in the open. Admit it freely. Talk about it with others. Get their advice on how to overcome it. Examine the reasons underlying it. Once you stop trying to hide it, you'll find it much easier to overcome.

5. Cultivate a sense of humor. Learn to laugh at yourself and your fears. It doesn't pay, you know, to take life – or yourself – too seriously. That was one of the devices Lincoln used to overcome fear.

6. In relations with others, remember that they are subject to the same emotions, the same motivation, the same doubts and worries, that affect you. They really want and need what you have to offer – your sympathy, your kindness, your thoughtfulness.

7. Stop thinking so much about yourself. Begin by trying every day to perform a deed of helpfulness for someone else. You'll soon find that in every way you are far more blessed with strength and courage and fortitude than you realized.

8. Above all, remember that you are never alone. You have the promise, in which you can trust utterly and completely, that a *Greater Power* is with you always to lend you His strength. Learn to rely on that Power, replenishing your spiritual forces through prayer and meditation. Faith in the Divine Power will give you faith in yourself.

Recipe for An Attractive Personality

1. Constructive mental attitude.
2. Flexibility.
3. Sincerity of purpose.
4. Promptness of decision.
5. Courtesy.
6. Pleasant tone of voice.
7. The habit of smiling.
8. Pleasant facial expression.
9. Tactfulness.
10. Tolerance.
11. Frankness of manner and speech.
12. A keen sense of humor.
13. Faith in Infinite Intelligence.
14. A sense of justice.
15. Appropriateness of words.
16. Emotional control.
17. Alertness of interest.
18. Effective speech.
19. Versatility.
20. Fondness for people.
21. Control of temper.
22. Hope and ambition.
23. Temperance.
24. Patience.
25. Humility of heart.
26. Appropriateness of personal adornment.
27. Good showmanship.
28. Clean sportsmanship.
29. Ability to shake hands properly.
30. Personal magnetism.

Southern Hospitality: A Form of a Pleasing Personality

I am very grateful for being raised in the South; Charleston, South Carolina, to be exact. Admittedly, I didn't always embrace my Southern roots because of the oppression my ancestors experienced while living in the South. As a teenager in the early eighties, I noticed the inequalities that existed between blacks and whites, and when I left my hometown, I vowed never to live there again.

A combination of maturity, my brother Gary's influence, and the study of Napoleon Hill's principles for over two decades helped me to look for and embrace the positive aspects of my experience of being raised in the South. In doing so, I discovered a thing called "Southern Hospitality." This is a phrase used to describe the idea that residents of the Southern United States are particularly warm and welcoming to visitors. Southern hospitality includes proper local etiquette, for example, calling one "sir" or "ma'am," opening doors for ladies, and inviting one to church functions. These customs may be seen as odd or even offensive by people not from the South; but they are meant as expressions of traditionally warm greetings.

Expressing these customs has caused me to stand out from the crowd in many situations—education, career, personal and business relationships, etc.—thus creating opportunities for me that might not have existed had I not possessed them.

You don't have to be from the South to develop and display a pleasing personality. All that is needed is a sincere heart, genuine love for others, and an appreciation for the differences that may exist between you and others.

—STEPHEN GRANT

Southern Shrimp & Grits

1 cup grits
4 slices bacon, cut into 1-inch pieces
1 tablespoon plus 1 teaspoon bacon drippings
1-1/2 cup smoked sausage, sliced in 1/4-inch pieces
3 tablespoons flour
1/2 teaspoon browning and seasoning sauce
1 cup water
1 medium sweet onion, diced
1-2 pounds shrimp, peeled, de-veined, washed, and dried with a hand towel
1/2 tablespoon seasoned salt

Cook grits according to directions on the package. The consistency of the grits should be thick.

In a sauce pan, fry bacon until it is brown. Remove the bacon from the pan. Retain bacon drippings.

Brown sausage in same pan. Remove sausage and discard drippings.

Mix flour, browning and seasoning sauce, and 1 tablespoon bacon drippings in a measuring cup. Blend until it is a smooth paste. Add water and set aside.

Clean residue from the sauce pan and return to stove. Sauté onion with 1 teaspoon bacon drippings over medium heat until golden.

Season shrimp with seasoned salt and add to pan. Sauté shrimp until it begins to turn pink.

Add bacon, sausage and the flour mixture and bring to a boil. Reduce the heat to low, place a lid on the sauce pan, and simmer for about 20 minutes, then remove from heat.

Serve grits in a wide soup bowl. Add a pat of butter and spoon shrimp along with the gravy on top.

I am a native of Charleston, South Carolina. I am who I am today because of my personal relationship with God, my brother's influence, and Napoleon Hill's success principles. Exposure to the three aforementioned influences empowers me to spend the rest of my life educating others, particularly young adults, about how to use the greatest gift from God, their minds. The mind is powerful, and proper conditioning will help you to achieve God's purpose for your life.

First Impressions are Lasting

The principle of a Pleasing Personality has been a great asset for me. I use it in many ways: I cultivate the habit of harmony within myself and others; the habit of looking for the good in others; the habits of going the extra mile and personal initiative; the habit of smiling when speaking; the habit of controlling my emotions; the habit of controlling not only my words and deeds, but also my thoughts; and the habit of a proper handshake, with enthusiasm, in a spirit of sincere friendship. Most importantly, I also strive for a positive mental attitude, which comprises many positive characteristics, like courage, faith, generosity, good common sense, hope, initiative, integrity, kindliness, optimism, tact, and tolerance.

What is the second best thing you can do with your lips? Smile! A smile makes you beautiful and it makes the person you smiled at happy. Happiness is a key ingredient to staying young! Courtesy is free. Let's strive to be nicer to those around us. Smiling at everyone we meet is an easy way to share our joy and happiness with others. By being courteous and friendly, we become richer in spirit.

Remember this always:

   Love makes our friends a little dearer

   Joy makes our hearts a little lighter

   Faith makes our paths a little clearer

   Hope makes our lives a little brighter

   Peace brings us all a little nearer

May your days be blessed with life's special treasures.

—POLY YAP

Simple and Nutritious Toaster Oven Chicken

- 2 chicken drumsticks, skinless
- 2 potatoes, peeled and diced
- 2 onions, peeled and cut vertically into 8 wedges
- 2 carrots, peeled and sliced
- 1 head cauliflower, chopped into 1-inch pieces
- 2 teaspoons chicken stock powder, or 1 chicken bouillon cube, crushed
- 1/4 teaspoon salt
- 1/4 teaspoon pepper

Preheat toaster oven to 350 degrees.

Place chicken into a 4-inch by 8-inch loaf pan.

Add potatoes, onions, carrots and cauliflower.

Sprinkle chicken stock powder, salt, and pepper evenly over the top.

Cover loaf pan with aluminum foil and bake for 15 minutes.

Turn off heat but leave pan inside to bake another 30 minutes before serving.

As an administrative employee cultivating a Pleasing Personality, my life has changed for the better. Not only do my colleagues and friends think I have likable qualities that enable me to motivate others to be better people, but also I think this will help me achieve my personal definite major purpose and serve in an active and successful mastermind alliance. I believe I am mentally, emotionally, spiritually, and physically sound, and this belief gives me a pleasant demeanor.

Recipe Notes

6. Personal Initiative

Personal Initiative requires you to have the capacity to concentrate your full attention upon one task at a time coupled with patience and persistence. The perfect recipes for this principle are the ones that require you to sustain your purpose until you have realized the outcome. I have selected two nut roll recipes that will make you feel as if you have completed a marathon when you finish. And, your family and friends will award you the gold medal for making these treats especially for them to enjoy.

- Judith Williamson

Nut Rolls
(makes six) Recipe by Izzy Kaptur

(Recipe can be doubled)

Dough:

8 cups flour

2 cups scalded milk (I use whole milk), let cool

1 cup sugar

2 cakes or two packets yeast

1 lb. margarine (I use Imperial). This is 4 sticks.

6 egg yolks, beaten

Mix flour, sugar and margarine together like pie crust. Dissolve yeast in lukewarm milk. Add a little sugar (1 tablespoon is sufficient) to the milk mixture in order to proof yeast. Let sit until foamy. Add beaten egg yolks to the milk mixture. Add liquid to flour gradually. Knead until hands come clean, adding a little extra flour if necessary. Form into a ball. Wrap in wax paper and put in refrigerator overnight. Meanwhile make the filling.

Filling:

1 ½ lbs. finely chopped nuts.

½ small jar honey

2 cups sugar

1 ½ sticks melted margarine (I use Imperial)

6 egg whites

Mix all the ingredients together except for the egg whites. Beat the chilled eggs whites until stiff in a glass bowl. Fold into nut mixture.

Preparation:

Cut dough into six pieces. Take out one piece at a time. Roll out thin on a flour dusted surface. Fill and roll up into a roll. Place on ungreased cookie sheet. Let rise for one hour. Bake at 350 degrees for 40 to 45 minutes. I alternate baking sheets in the oven after ½ the baking time to brown the nut rolls uniformly. Frost while warm with glaze.

Glaze:

Confectioners Sugar – 1 box sifted

Milk – ¼ to 1/3 cup heated

Vanilla – 1 tsp.

Mix together well and frost nut rolls while warm.

Personal Initiative

> **"** ...the power that inspires the completion of that which one begins. **"**
> -Napoleon Hill

Recipe for Goal Setting

Four important things to keep in mind when setting a goal:

(a) *Write down your goal.* You will crystallize your thinking. The very act of thinking as you write will create an indelible impression in your memory.

(b) *Give yourself a deadline.* Specify a time for achieving your objective. This is important in motivating you: to set out in the direction of your goal and keep moving towards it.

(c) *Set your standards high.* Now there seems to be a direct relationship between ease in achieving a goal and the strength of your motives.

And the higher you set your major goal, generally speaking, the more concentrated will be the effort you make to achieve it.

The reason-logic will make it mandatory that you at least aim at an intermediate objective as well as an immediate one. So aim higher. And then have immediate and intermediate steps leading towards its achievement.

This may stimulate your thinking! Where will you be and what will you be doing ten years from today if you keep doing what you are doing now?

(d) *Aim high.* It is a peculiar thing that no more effort is required to aim high in life, to demand prosperity and abundance, than is required to accept misery and poverty.

You have to be bold enough to ask of life more than you may, right now, feel you are worth because it is an observable fact that people tend to rise to meet demands that are put upon them.

While it is exceedingly desirable that you blueprint your program from beginning to end, this is not always feasible. One doesn't always know all the answers between the beginning of a great enterprise or journey and its ending. But if you know where you are and where you want to be and you start from where you are to get to where you want to be, you will, if you keep properly motivated, move forward step by step until you get there yourself.

Recipe for the Development of Leadership

1. The first step essential in the development of initiative and leadership is that of forming the habit of prompt and firm decision. All successful people have a certain amount of decision. The man who wavers between two or more half-baked and more or less vague notions of what he wants to do generally ends by doing nothing.

2. It is not enough to have a definite chief aim and a definite plan for its achievement, even though the plan may be perfectly practical and you may have all the necessary ability to carry it through successfully—you must have more than these—you must actually take the initiative and put the wheels of your plan into motion and keep them turning until your goal has been reached.

3. Study those whom you know to be failures (you'll find them all around you) and observe that, without a single exception, they lack the firmness of decision, even in matters of the smallest importance. Such people usually "talk" a great deal, but they are very short on performance. "Deeds, not words" should be the motto of the man who intends to succeed in life, no matter what may be his calling, or what he has selected as his definite chief aim.

4. Prominent and successful leaders are always people who reach decisions quickly, yet it is not to be assumed that quick decisions are always advisable. There are circumstances calling for deliberation, the study of facts connected with the intended decision, etc. However, after all available facts have been gathered and organized, there is no excuse for delaying decision, and the person who practices the habit of such delay cannot become an effective leader until he masters this shortcoming.

Poteca

2 pkg. active dry yeast

1 T. sugar

1 c. milk, scaled and cooled

½ c. lard or margarine

½ c. sugar

3 eggs

1 tsp. vanilla

4-½ c. all purpose flour

½ tsp. salt

Filling:

1 c. milk

½ c. honey

½ c. sugar

½ c. firmly packed brown sugar

¼ butter or margarine

6 c. ground walnuts

1 tsp. cinnamon

1 tsp. vanilla

2 eggs

Combine scaled milk, yeast and 1 tablespoon sugar; set aside. In large bowl cream lard and ½ cup sugar. Add eggs; beat well. Add yeast mixture, vanilla, 2 cups flour and salt; combine thoroughly. Gradually add 2 more cups flour stirring until mixture forms a ball. Use remaining ½ cup flour to lightly knead dough; dough will be soft and slightly sticky. Place dough in greased bowl. Cover and let rise in warm place until light and double in size, about 2 hours.

In large saucepan heat 1 cup milk, honey, sugar, brown sugar and butter to boiling. Stir in walnuts, cinnamon and vanilla. Cook 5 to 10 minutes longer, stirring constantly. Cool to lukewarm. Beat in eggs, one at a time, until thoroughly blended.

Punch down dough. Flour a clean large surface generously. Divide dough into 2 equal parts. Place half in center of floured surface and roll into rectangle about 30x20 inches, rolling as thin as possible without tearing dough. Spread cooled filling over dough. Roll dough jelly style fashion starting at longest side. Carefully transfer roll to greased cookie sheet and shape into a circle, seam side down. Repeat process with other half of dough. Cover rings and let rise in warm place 30 minutes. Heat oven to 325 degrees. Bake for 40 to 45 minutes or until dark golden brown.

Note: Once you make this, your family will request it often. It is worth the extra effort for the praise you will receive.

Achieve Your Dreams

My recipe for success embraces Hill's sixth key to success, Personal Initiative. Personal initiative drives you from within. Follow this recipe and achieve your dreams!

First, identify your true desires. Simply ask yourself what it is that you desire. Address mental, emotional, physical, financial, and spiritual desires.

Second, find your inner motivation. What drives you to action? Reflect on your desires. What will the attainment of your desires bring you? How will your life be better when you attain these desires? Does this reflection spark your inner motivation? Reflect on what your life would be like if you do not attain your desires. Does this reflection spark your inner motivation as well?

Third, make the attainment of the object of your desires real. The more you believe that you can achieve your desires, the more you will find the strength to continue doing what it takes to attain them.

Fourth, use your inner motivation to drive personal achievement. Keep your inner motivation strong. Repeat steps two and three often to continually elevate your inner motivation.

Fifth, celebrate your personal achievements. As you attain your desires—and you will attain them— celebrate. Revel in the attainment of your desires, let the attainment of one desire feed your inner motivation for the attainment of yet another desire, and another, and another. Have fun through all of this. Life is *wonderful*!

—DIANE MARIE BYRD

Sauerkraut, Kielbasa, and Potato Noodles

3/4 stick of butter (6 tablespoons)
1 large yellow onion, diced
1 large can (27 ounces) shredded sauerkraut
60 ounces water (use empty kraut can)
1 pound kielbasa or smoked sausage, cut into 1/2-inch slices
1/2 cup ketchup
2 large potatoes
3 eggs
1 cup all-purpose flour, plus a little more

In a large, deep skillet, melt butter and sauté onion until translucent. Add sauerkraut, 1 can of water, sausage, and ketchup. Cover and simmer 1 1/2 to 2 hours. Start potato noodles after 1 hour.

Take a large deep pot and fill 2/3 full with water. Bring water to a boil. While waiting for water to boil, prepare the noodle mixture. Peel potatoes and place in cold water (this keeps them from turning color). Hand grate each potato to a fine, mushy texture. Add eggs and stir to blend. Add flour and stir to blend. The best potato noodle dough is not too stiff and not too loose.

Tip: The dough will appear somewhat sticky. Add more flour in small amounts as needed to make the dough stiff enough that it does not break apart when dropped from a spoon.

Drop dough by spoonfuls into boiling water (each spoonful will be about 1/8 cup). As the dough drops, it will stretch into noodles. Boil noodles until they float, about 20 minutes after the last noodle is dropped. Drain water and combine potato noodles with sauerkraut mixture.

In the mid-1980's, I read **Think and Grow Rich** *by Napoleon Hill. As I finished the book, I remember experiencing an emotional wave that brought me to tears. I finally understood why I was where I was—mentally, emotionally, physically, financially, and spiritually—and I knew life could be even better. I internalized the lessons of that book and applied them to all aspects of my life. I went from being the consummate procrastinator to one who consistently uses personal initiative. I found the inner strength to achieve amazing things in life. I love wholly, live graciously, and am thankful every day for all that life offers.*

Napoleon Hill

7. Positive Mental Attitude

Having a **Positive Mental Attitude** requires you to look at life from multiple perspectives. Being open and accepting of more than just our personal point of view is a trait that Napoleon Hill identified as tolerance. Being tolerant assists an individual in the development of **PMA** since it widens our outlook. These two recipes below can widen us too if we are not careful! Both are simple, special treats that guests will ask you to serve time and time again.

- Judith Williamson

Marshmallow Fruit Salad

2 c. mandarin oranges, drained
2 c. pineapple tidbits, drained
2 c. sour cream
2 c. shredded coconut
2 c. pecans or walnuts, chopped
1 large bag white miniature marshmallows
1 jar salad cherries, drained and sliced in half

In a large bowl, combine the oranges, pineapple, sour cream, coconut, pecans, marshmallows, and cherries. Mix well. Chill.

Note: Always popular around any holiday.

Bread Pudding with Whiskey Sauce

3-4 slices white bread
(number of slices can vary)
because of the size. I suggest 1/2 a loaf) - you can use French bread as well
4 T. sugar
3 and 1/2 cups milk, whole milk is best
4 eggs, separated
1 tbsp. vanilla
pinch salt
1 - 2 sticks sticks butter (1/2 to 1 cup)
1/2 tsp. cinnamon
raisins, optional

1. Break bread into overproof dish (1 and 1/2 quart at least - I use an oblong 9x13 baking pan).
2. Soften bread with small amount of milk.
3. Beat sugar and egg yolks.
4. Add milk, and stir well.
5. Add vanilla, cinnamon and salt.
6. Pour milk mixture over bread. Fold in raisins, if used.
7. Cut butter into chunks and fold in.
8. Place dish in pan of water and bake at 300 degrees for 40-50 minutes or until silver knife inserted comes out clean.
9. Make meringue adding 2 level tablespoons sugar to each egg white. Beat until stiff peaks form. Spread on top of pudding and return to 350 degree oven until brown (browning in slow oven prevents falling). Check it every 30 seconds to one minute or so. It can burn quickly, as meringue does, so check it often. If you do not like meringue, leave it off, and serve the bread pudding with vanilla ice cream and whiskey sauce – or just with the whiskey sauce.

Whiskey Sauce:
1/2 cup sugar
1/4 cup water
1 stick butter

Can double or triple recipe easily.

Cook until dissolved. Remove from heat, add whiskey to individual taste.

Positive Mental Attitude

> *"...is the right mental attitude in all circumstances."*
> -Napoleon Hill

Recipe for Controlling Your Mental Attitude

Your mental attitude can be conditioned and controlled by a number of factors, among them, these:

1. By a BURNING DESIRE for the attainment of a definite purpose based upon one or more of the nine basic motives which activate all human endeavor, the first three of which are, the emotion of love, the emotion of sex, and the desire for financial gain.

2. By close association with people who are themselves positive-minded and who inspire others to think and act in terms of a positive mental attitude. Every person who aspires to become a top-ranking success should have one or more "pace makers"—people whose achievements and characters he admires—whom he endeavors to emulate, to overtake, and even to excel. Hero worship can be very beneficial if one chooses the right persons as heroes.

3. By auto-suggestion through which the mind is constantly being given definite directives until it attracts only that for which these directives call. This procedure should be carried on both silently and orally. One very successful actor goes over his lines many times daily while looking at himself in a mirror. A successful lawyer addresses an imaginary court and jury many times before he goes into court with his cases. And a clergyman of national prominence delivers his sermons to himself, in front of a mirror, many times before he goes into the pulpit of his church.

4. By the habit of daily prayer in which one expresses gratitude for the blessings he already possesses instead of asking for more; requesting instead more wisdom with which to make better use of his present riches. This habit perhaps ranks at the top of the list in importance because it is one in which the full powers of one's religious belief can be strengthened and made to serve whatever ends one may choose.

5. You have within you a sleeping giant who is ready to be awakened and directed by you to the performance of any sort of service you desire. And when you wake up some morning and find yourself on the success beam and in the upper brackets of success you will wonder why you had not sooner discovered that you had all the makings of a big success.

A Sweet Dessert – Contentment!

The richest man in all the world lives in Happy Valley. He is rich in values that endure, in things he cannot lose—things that provide him with contentment, sound health, peace of mind, and harmony within his soul.

Here is an inventory of his riches and how he acquired them:

"I found happiness by helping others to find it."

"I found sound health by living temperately and eating only the food my body requires to maintain itself."

"I hate no man, envy no man, but love and respect all mankind."

"I am engaged in a labor of love with which I mix play generously; therefore, I seldom grow tired."

"I pray daily, not for more riches, but for more wisdom with which to recognize, embrace, and enjoy the great abundance of riches I already possess."

"I speak no name save only to honor it, and I slander no man for any cause whatsoever."

"I ask no favors of anyone except the privilege of sharing my blessings with all who desire them."

"I am on good terms with my conscience; therefore, it guides me accurately in everything I do."

"I have more material wealth than I need because I am free from greed and covet only those things I can use constructively while I live. My wealth comes from those whom I have benefited by sharing my blessings."

"The estate of Happy Valley which I own is not taxable. It exists mainly in my own mind, in intangible riches that cannot be assessed for taxation or appropriated except by those who adopt my way of life. I created this estate over a lifetime of effort by observing nature's laws and forming habits to conform with them."

POSITIVE MENTAL ATTITUDE

Positivity is Infectious

On a cold, dreary winter morning, we were assembling for our quarterly, 7:00 A.M. meeting. The tone in the room was less than exhilarating. Although most of the people there appreciated our efforts to keep them informed, they would have preferred a different venue and time. Right at 7:00, a new face entered the room, walked to the front row, and sat down. That, in and of itself, was a rarity. The seats in the front two rows were avoided like the plague. I couldn't help but notice how the other people in the room were fixed on her movement and shared my astonishment. Since all attention was on this new person, I opened the meeting by asking her how she was doing. She replied, without hesitation and with a smile on her face, "Wonderful!"

Instantly, the tone of the room changed. People sat up in their chairs. Facial expressions turned from burdened frowns to welcoming smiles. I had an open and receptive audience in front of me and I felt energized. That morning, Gloria's actions had actually influenced the mental attitude of the people in the room. We had a terrific meeting.

I made it a point to get to know Gloria better. I learned her husband was suffering from kidney failure and would die without a donor. After a long struggle, they lost the battle, but despite the enormous pain, Gloria always maintained a profound faith in God and a positive mental attitude.

I've seen how living life with a positive mental attitude backed with applied faith can help a person deal with despair, anguish, and great pain and infect the multitudes in a good way. I am blessed to have had the opportunity to meet and get to know such a special person.

—PHIL BARLOW

Best Ever Chicken Salad

1 cup Miracle Whip or mayonnaise
1 cup sour cream
2 tablespoons lemon juice
1 -1/2 tablespoons salt
4 cups cooked chicken, chopped
1/2 cup pecans, chopped
4 slices bacon, cooked and crumbled
2 cups celery, chopped
1 small can (4 ounces) mushrooms, drained

In a small bowl, whisk together Miracle Whip, sour cream, lemon juice, and salt.

Combine other ingredients in a separate, larger bowl. Pour Miracle Whip mixture over all. Toss lightly.

Serve on a bed of lettuce with tomato slices.

In 1977, I was on a dead-end street. I hated to get up every morning for another 12-hour day of drudgery. One day, I found a used and abused paperback copy of **Think and Grow Rich**, *picked it up and started reading. Call it luck, coincidence or even fate: finding and reading that book changed my life forever. I couldn't get my mind off the principle of Definiteness of Purpose. The more I thought about my purpose in life, the clearer the picture got. Action took over and in a short number of years, I rose from the ranks of the uninspired to having the privilege of leading one of the most successful manufacturing companies in north Georgia.*

POSITIVE MENTAL ATTITUDE

You Can Choose Your Life

Napoleon Hill said, "If you put your mind to work with a positive mental attitude and believe that success is your right, your belief will guide you unerringly toward whatever your definition of success might be."

Now I can't imagine what I would do if I didn't have PMA. When I do something, I always believe I can do it, and that I am the right one to get it done. Working hard on what you are doing with a positive mental attitude, you will achieve your purpose.

In August 2007, my employer, the Napoleon Hill World Learning Center, held a certification course on a cruise to the Bahamas. Before we left, I searched the U.S. Immigration Web site and printed out the document that would prove I am legal to go to the Bahamas and come back to the United States without going to an embassy. But when we checked in, the official asked me to wait there, and told me I couldn't board. I showed them the document; they said they hadn't seen it before and needed time to confirm it.

I told myself things should be okay, since I had planned ahead and found the right documentation before I arrived. After two hours—just five minutes before the ship set sail—the cruise line received confirmation from the immigration office, and let me board the ship.

Working hard is necessary, but without PMA you can't maximize your success.

—GUANG CHEN

"ALAN"

Tofu Balls

- 1 package (16 ounces) firm tofu
- 4 dried shiitake mushrooms
- 1 small turnip, peeled
- 2 tablespoons green snow-peas, finely chopped
- 2 tablespoons carrots, finely chopped
- 2 tablespoons water chestnuts, finely chopped
- 1 teaspoon salt
  pinch ground white pepper
- 2 eggs
- 32 ounces vegetable oil for deep frying

Drain and press tofu to remove excess water.
Soak mushrooms in water until softened, about 30 minutes. Discard mushroom stems and finely chop mushroom caps.
Shred turnip and squeeze in a cloth to remove excess fluid.
Crumble tofu in a large bowl.
Add turnip, mushroom, peas, carrots, and water chestnuts and mix well.
Add salt and pepper to taste.
Beat eggs and add to tofu. Mix thoroughly.
Heat about 1 inch vegetable oil in a heavy skillet for deep frying.
Scoop about 2 tablespoons tofu mixture and roll between your palms to create walnut-sized balls.
Deep-fry tofu balls until golden brown; drain on paper towels.
Serve immediately.

I come from China and have been in the United States for three years. After studying for two years here, I had a choice to make: go back to China or renew my visa and work here. I love this country and really want to live and work here for several years. But nobody believed I could get a new visa in time. They said, "It's impossible, you're wasting your time." I said, "Stop, I don't need any negative advice." I spent almost a full month preparing the visa renewal application with my employer and attorney, and it was approved! Now I am working at the Napoleon Hill World Learning Center and enjoying the life I was positive I could have.

POSITIVE MENTAL ATTITUDE

Simple Recipe for Happiness

Each morning when you wake up, thank God that you are getting to start another day. Put a smile on your face. Smile at the first person that you come into contact with. Keep that smile on your face and use it through your day. Happiness is contagious; note all the smiles that you receive in return. Repeat this recipe every day for the rest of your life.

Being happy is a state of mind. Keep a Positive Mental Attitude and a smile and you will be a happier person.

—WILMA JACKSON

Nothing great was ever achieved without a positive mental attitude.

Character is accurately reflected in one's mental attitude.

A positive mind finds a way it can be done, a negative mind looks for all the ways it can't be done.

—NAPOLEON HILL

Mrs. Sees' Fudge

4 1/2 cups sugar
1 large can evaporated milk
1/2 pound margarine or butter, softened
18 ounces semisweet chocolate chips
1 jar (10 ounces) marshmallow fluff
2 teaspoons vanilla
2-1/2 cups walnuts or pecans, chopped

In a pot, bring sugar and evaporated milk to a boil. Boil for 10 minutes, stirring constantly.

Put margarine, chocolate chips, and marshmallow into a large mixing bowl. Pour milk into the bowl and beat mixture for 15 minutes.

Add vanilla and nuts. Mix until evenly distributed.

Pour fudge into a greased 9-inch by 13-inch pan. Let sit until firm.

For a special touch, add whole nuts on top or on individual pieces.

I am now retired after working for the same manufacturing plant for 46 years. I always enjoyed my work and the people I worked with. My recipe for happiness has always given me good rapport with people both at work and at home.

Win The World In Three Steps

I was very much moved by this simple, but most profound principle, which in itself is a complete formula for success. As a human being, often I think and act in negative thoughts and actions, but as soon as I realize my negativity, I stick to the principle of positivism and correct my negativity boldly, with open heart and without hesitation.

On few occasions, however, due to over-positivity, I found myself in losing situations with monetary losses. Therefore, I thought it over again and again and invented my own small formula of positive success, which helps one look squarely into the eyes of problems and gives the best possible result. This is my "Triple-A" formula of success:

A is for Attitude. A is for Aim. A is for Action.

Dr. Hill says that one should "teach the subject which you want to master." Therefore, I told this formula to my family and friends and asked their feelings about the result it produced in their lives. It was amazing for them too, because it is short and easy to remember, but versatile in application.

I started lecturing and writing my success philosophy to teach and learn more and more, and soon I became noted in my city and suburbs. Meanwhile, I received an invitation to write a book on my Triple-A success philosophy, *Teen Kadam Me Duniya Jeeto (Win The World In Three Steps)*. It was certainly the deep-rooted Positive Mental Attitude and nothing else which turned my ideas on paper into a published book of 200 pages, which is hitting the stands of many bookshops in India.

—RAJIV KAPOOR

Benarsi Thandai (Indian Dry-Fruit Drink)

6 cups water
1 cup sugar (or to taste)
1 tablespoon almonds
1 tablespoon sunflower seeds, raw, hulled
1/2 tablespoon poppy seeds
1/2 tablespoon anise seed
1/2 teaspoon ground cardamom
1 teaspoon peppercorns
1 teaspoon rose or orange flower water

Dissolve sugar in 2 cups water. Set aside.

Combine remaining ingredients with 2 cups water. Set aside to stand for at least 2 hours.

Grind soaked spice mix to a very fine paste in a food processor or blender.

Place a double layer of cheesecloth in a strainer and set over a large pitcher. Pour the spice paste through the cheesecloth. Press with the back of a spoon, extracting as much liquid as possible.

Add remaining water, a little at a time, to extract more of the flavor.

Pour some of the extracted juice back into the cheesecloth and press again. Repeat several times to extract as much flavor as possible. (Save the paste—excellent in curry dishes.)

Add sugar water to extracted liquid in pitcher. Mix well. Chill for at least 1-2 hours before serving. You may need to give the drink a stir before pouring.

Serve chilled or over ice. Sprinkle some rose petals over each serving (optional).

I am "Made In India." I was fortunate that my parents educated me at the best institutes. I jumped into business with the assistance of my elder brother, and was very successful. In the 1980s, I found **Success Through a Positive Mental Attitude**. *I was transfixed, and when finished, I continued studying the rest of Napoleon Hill's books. In 2002, I organized a celebration of W. Clement Stone's 100th birthday in India, including feeding the hungry street people in recognition of Stone's lifetime of positive acts. It was a U-turn in my career, which transformed me from a successful businessman to an international motivator and bestselling author.*

POSITIVE MENTAL ATTITUDE

Switch to Your Positive Self

One of the most essential habits to possess in life is to have a positive mental attitude. Ever since I completed the Science of Success program in 2005 and inculcated the Napoleon Hill Principles into my thought, I have always used auto-suggestion to stay "above the line." The danger of dropping into negativity could easily explode into great calamity.

In December 2006, I came to work in Australia. I was off to Canberra to undertake a project from Melbourne. A new job, a new country, and a new climate—my life spun around completely. It was easy to feel dejected by the turn of events. I was having great difficulty comprehending the Aussie accent, so Canberra seemed hardly the place for me. I missed my family back home. There was a feeling of emptiness in my mind, and I wondered if that was what insanity is like.

In the moment of need, Dr. Napoleon Hill's image came up from my subconscious mind. The first thing to do was to have equilibrium in my body and thought, stay above the line (positive mental attitude), and keep my focus (controlled attention). I revisited my definite major purpose of coming to Australia, thought about my ultimate goal, and many of the wonderful benefits of achieving that goal flashed through my mind. Every negative was substituted with two positive thoughts. I had faith (applied faith) that I would feel better.

After I got myself settled in, guess what other principles began to emerge? Pleasing personality, mastermind alliance, going the extra mile, accurate thinking, learning from adversity, and cosmic habitforce. Amazing, right? I intend to maintain this positive state of mind, and switch it on as often as I want or need. Thanks to Dr. Hill, and thanks to Napoleon Hill Associates in Malaysia.

—GEORGE LEE

Bo Bo Cha Cha

Enjoy the sweetness after a tough day.

- 2 quarts water
- 1 medium size yam, cubed
- 3 to 4 small sweet potatoes, cubed
- 4 pieces pandan leaves (tie into a knot)
- 1/4 cup sago or corn starch
- 1-2 cups coconut milk (from 1 coconut)

Boil water in a medium pot and add yam and sweet potatoes.

After a few minutes, add pandan leaves.

Pour 2/3 of the coconut milk into the pot. Let it boil on low heat for 10 minutes.

Mix sago or corn starch with 1/4 cup cold water, then stir into the pot.

Boil for another 10 minutes, or until yam and potatoes are done to your liking. Add a small amount of water and coconut milk if sauce is too thick. Reserve some coconut milk for serving.

Serve in small bowls, with a little coconut milk on top.

I was born in Selangor, Malaysia, and I have always sought to live a better spiritual life. My first child, who is a test tube baby, was diagnosed with heart complications at the age of two. We and the pediatrician hoped she would improve, but after six months, our hopes were dashed. In July 2004 she underwent surgery. My heart nearly broke when I handed my daughter to the doctors. Since then, Priscilla has grown stronger, and my wife and I had our second daughter in 2005 the normal way. Dr. Hill's principles came to us in 2005, one year after Priscilla was born. This philosophy is the answer for me to live a better life, especially to deal with adversity.

Positive Mental Attitudes Create Positive Lives

As a young boy, I always found myself in trouble at school, from talking and disrupting class to turning in homework late. As a result, I hated school, I hated life, and I felt everyone was against me. I was told over and over that my attitude was bad. I was always feeling down and looking down.

I learned to avoid trouble as a young adult, but my attitude became even worse. My world included the Vietnam war, race riots, discrimination, and the assassinations of Martin Luther King, Malcolm X, and the Kennedys. I had a terrible case of Negative Mental Attitude.

When I was 24, I attended a real estate seminar by Jim Rohn. He said, "for things to change, you have to change," and, "life is not about liking it, but about learning it." He suggested I read ***Think and Grow Rich***.

As I studied Dr. Hill's book, I learned of Positive Mental Attitude. I learned to set goals and look for opportunities. I changed my attitude from negative to positive. Then, to my amazement, everyone and everything around me became positive. The more I learned, the more I began looking up and feeling better. The things I once hated, I now loved.

Positive Mental Attitude means having a definite purpose in life, and expecting to accomplish it using all of the 17 success principles daily. When you seek abundance, you will find it. You are the captain of your ship, creator of your destiny. Look up. There is magic in looking up. There is a silver lining in every cloud. Look up as your attitude becomes your gratitude. Look up often.

—Fred Wikkeling

Pound Cake

An excellent Wikkeling family recipe.

- 1 pound butter
- 2 cups sugar
- 3 cups flour
- 1 teaspoon baking powder
- 6 eggs
- 1 can sweetened condensed milk
- 1 teaspoon vanilla extract

Preheat oven to 350 degrees.

Cream butter and sugar together.

Mix flour and baking powder, then add to butter mixture.

Add 1 egg, then a little condensed milk, mixing well after each. Continue alternating until all eggs and milk are incorporated.

Add vanilla and mix well.

Pour batter into greased Bundt pan.

Bake for 1 hour or until skewer or toothpick comes out clean.

Since my transformation from an unhappy, rebellious youth, I have become a successful real estate entrepreneur, inspirational lecturer, and writer. I apply three decades of self-achievement experience to help my students and readers achieve their dreams by living their lives to the fullest. I have been honored to become a certified instructor for the Napoleon Hill Foundation, and I spread Dr. Hill's philosophy as widely as I can. Currently I live in San Jose, California, with my wife and two children.

Recipe Notes:

"A negative mind spawns only negative ideas."

8. Enthusiasm

Enthusiasm is said to be faith in action. It is powerful because it can transmute failures and temporary defeats into successes because of the power of faith. **Enthusiasm** needs to be controlled enthusiasm to be of value. Uncontrolled enthusiasm does not produce stable results. The two recipes for this principle resemble dishes that people generally do not get enthusiastic about. But, with controlled enthusiasm and the right recipe, the results are delicious. The Festive Fruit Cake recipe is a guaranteed winner and will definitely challenge people to take back their negative opinions about fruit cakes. Sliced thin and served with tea or coffee, no one can resist the nutty cherry flavor. Next, the deviled egg recipe is one that requires enthusiasm in boiling and peeling the eggs to make the end result perfectly acceptable and buffet ready. However, if all else fails, this recipe can be easily transmuted into the perfect egg salad canapé that everyone will enjoy too! Just spread it freely on melba toast or toast points and no one will suspect that what was supposed to be deviled eggs morphed into something else!

- Judith Williamson

Deviled Eggs

1 dozen eggs, cooked in salted water, chilled, and peeled

½ c. Miracle Whip salad dressing or mayonnaise

1 T. prepared mustard

3 T. sweet pickle relish

1 small can deviled ham

1 T. prepared horseradish, optional

salt and pepper to taste

black or green olives, sliced for garnish

parsley springs, for garnish

paprika

Cut cooked, chilled, and peeled eggs in half lengthwise. Remove the yolks. In a medium bowl combine the yolks, salad dressing or mayonnaise, mustard, sweet pickle relish, deviled ham, salt and pepper, and prepared horseradish (optional). Mash well with fork to blend until smooth. Use a teaspoon to fill the cavities of the egg whites. Garnish each with sliced olives, parsley, and sprinkle lightly with paprika, if desired. Arrange on a serving plate. Chill.

Note: A real hit at any function. Hardest part is peeling the eggs!

Enthusiasm

> " ...is faith in action. "
> -Napoleon Hill

How to Speak Enthusiastically

1. Talk loudly! This is particularly necessary if you are emotionally upset, if you are shaking inside when you stand before an audience, if you have "butterflies in your stomach."

2. Talk rapidly! You mind functions more quickly when you do. You can read two books with greater understanding in the time you now read one if you concentrate and read with rapidity.

3. Emphasize! Emphasize important words, words that are important to you or your listening audience—a word like *you,* for example.

4. Hesitate! When you talk rapidly, hesitate where there would be a period, comma, or other punctuation in the written word. Thus you employ the dramatic effect of silence. The mind of the person who is listening catches up with the thoughts you have expressed. Hesitation after a word which you wish to emphasize accentuates the emphasis.

5. Keep a smile in your voice! Thus in talking loudly and rapidly, you eliminate gruffness. You can put a smile in your voice by putting a smile on your face, a smile in your eyes.

6. Modulate! This is important if you are speaking for a long period. Remember, you can modulate both pitch and volume. You can speak loudly and intermittently change to a conversational tone and a lower pitch if you wish.

Inspire Enthusiasm

Your ability to inspire others is a blank check on the Bank of Life that you can fill in for whatever you desire. If you lack this ability, you can take steps to acquire it.

Here are some rules to adopt and follow:

1. Go out of your way to speak a kind word or render some useful service where it is not expected;
2. Modify your voice to convey a feeling of warmth and friendship to those you address;
3. Direct your conversation to subjects of the greatest interest to your listeners. Talk "with" them rather than "to" them. Consider the persons with whom you're conversing as the most interesting in the world, at least at that moment;
4. Soften your expression frequently with a smile as you speak;
5. Never, under any circumstances, use profanity or obscenity;
6. Keep your religious and political views to yourself;
7. Never ask a favor of anyone you haven't yourself helped at some time;
8. Be a good listener. Inspire others to speak freely. Remember that an ounce of optimism is worth a ton of pessimism;
9. Close each day with this prayer: "I ask not for more blessings, but more wisdom with which to make better use of the blessings I now possess. And give me, please, more understanding that I may occupy more space in the hearts of my fellow men by rendering more service tomorrow than I have rendered today."

ENTHUSIASM

Festive Fruit Cake

1 c. brazil nuts

2 c. walnuts

1 c. pecans

1 pound pitted dates

1 8-oz. jar red maraschino cherries, drained

¾ cup flour

¾ cup sugar

½ tsp. baking powder

½ tsp. salt

1 tsp. vanilla

3 eggs beaten very well

Cut large nuts in half, leaving small ones whole. Cut cherries and dates in half also, if desired. Place nuts, cherries and dates in large bowl. Add flour that has been sifted with baking powder, salt and sugar. Coat the fruit and nut mixture well with the dry ingredients. Add the vanilla to the well-beaten eggs. Eggs should be beaten for at least five minutes. Pour egg mixture over the floured mixture and blend well. Pour into a 9x5x3½ inch loaf pan which has been greased, lined with waxed paper and greased again. If desired, place about 3 or 4 green maraschino cherries on top for color. Bake for 1½ hours at 300 degrees. Store in a cool place. Top with Fruit Cake Glaze, if desired.

Fruit Cake Glaze

½ cup light corn syrup

¼ cup water

Combine ingredients in pan and bring to rolling boil. Remove from heat and cool to lukewarm. Brush over cooled fruit cake before or after storing.

Note: If you make this Festive Fruit Cake once, you will make it every year. Even if you don't like fruit cake, this recipe will become one of your all time favorites.

The Fuel That Creates Momentum

Everyday tasks can be things to look forward to with enthusiasm; fear and nervousness are replaced by happiness. Like love, it comes from the heart. If it is nurtured, enthusiasm will grow and become contagious to surrounding friends and colleagues.

I find it easy to get hyped up about certain things, and I spend my time pursuing what I'm enthusiastic about: family (5 kids and 17 grandkids), working with people (I'm currently helping a friend campaign for public office), and mission work, which helps the less fortunate at home and abroad.

I apply daily the 17 Principles of Success, which also helps build enthusiasm.

Masterminding with other successful people boosts my own passion for personal growth. When filled with enthusiasm, any doubt, fear, revenge, intolerance, and procrastination are put aside.

Like the recipes you find in this book, applied enthusiasm, when combined with the other principles, results in something really good at the end!

—Gaynell M. Larsen

Gay Gay's Orzo Salad

3 cups cooked orzo
1 bag (5–7 ounces) baby spinach
1 large bunch of fresh basil, chopped
1 sweet red pepper, diced
1/3 cup olive oil
 salt and pepper to taste
 Mrs. Dash's tomato and basil seasoning
2 cups cherry tomatoes, halved

Cook orzo in salted water and drain well. Set aside.

Break up spinach in microwavable bowl. Stir in basil and red pepper. Pour olive oil over spinach mixture.

Microwave until spinach is wilted (approximately 1-1/2 minutes).

Pour heated spinach mixture over cooked orzo and season to taste. I use salt and pepper and lots of Mrs. Dash's tomato and basil seasoning. You may also want to add more olive oil, if needed, at this time.

Serve hot, with cherry tomatoes added just before serving!

I live with my husband, David, in Floyd, Virginia, in the Blue Ridge Mountains. We have been successful small-business owners in the area for many years, and now sell rural land for-sale-by-owner. In 1992, we founded the non-profit Foundation for Amateur International Radio Service (FAIRS) to work with groups in less fortunate countries. We develop emergency radio communications systems and provide medical and equipment assistance. We direct the activities of the foundation and have a real passion for helping people.

ENTHUSIASM

Parenting with Enthusiasm

As I began to go through my recipes for this book, I came across handwritten recipes given to me by my husband's aunts before I married. (They knew I needed help.) Looking at their handwriting, I realized the time they took to write each recipe and to choose recipes that would be easy for a new bride. I reminisced about each aunt as I glanced at the recipes. I began to think about the thought and care going into everyday life for our loved ones.

Being a mother of three sons has always challenged me to adapt to everyday situations. With my first-born, I strived for perfection; with the second son I realized it was okay for his hands to get dirty; with my third, I started to relax and enjoy our moments together. Each has a totally different personality, so I always had to choose a different combination of principles to help each son reach his potential. Just as with a recipe, as you add each ingredient, it becomes more like the final product.

As I look back, I always had enthusiasm for parenting. Enthusiasm is "faith in action," according to Napoleon Hill. Each time I became discouraged, enthusiasm was always my motivator. Once I had enthusiasm, I continued to seek the best solution to achieve my goal. I believe many things in my life were achieved through a combination of success principles used with enthusiasm. Just like it takes more than one ingredient for a recipe to be tasty, success takes more than one principle of success, stirred vigorously with enthusiasm. I hope you will try Aunt Rose's recipe and remember the love and care that goes into your relationships. Always add enthusiasm as needed.

—GAYLE WASHAUSEN

Aunt Rose's Yum-Yum Coffee Cake

1/2 cup margarine
1 cup sugar
2 eggs
2 cups all-purpose flour
1 teaspoon baking soda
1 teaspoon baking powder
1/2 teaspoon salt
1 cup sour cream
1 teaspoon vanilla extract
Topping
1/3 cup brown sugar
1/4 cup white sugar
1 teaspoon cinnamon
3/4 cup pecans or walnuts, chopped

Preheat oven to 325 degrees.

Cream margarine and sugar. Add one egg and beat well. Add second egg and beat well.

Sift flour, baking soda, baking powder, and salt. Add half the dry ingredients to wet ingredients. Mix well. Add 1/2 cup sour cream and mix well. Add remaining dry ingredients and mix well. Add remaining sour cream and vanilla. Mix batter thoroughly.

Combine topping ingredients and mix well.

Put half of the batter in a greased 9-inch by 12-inch baking dish. Sprinkle half the topping over the batter. Pour remaining batter in, then sprinkle remaining topping on top.

Bake for 45 to 50 minutes.

I have been blessed to have three successful sons and a wonderful husband. Working at The Calumet Conference Center at Purdue University Calumet has given me opportunities to meet and work with many wonderfully people from different walks of life. Daily my life is enriched because of the work that I do and the people that I meet.

Recipe Notes

Napoleon Hill

9. Self-Discipline

Napoleon Hill says that no other single requirement for individual success is as important as self-discipline. Simply stated, self-discipline or self-control means taking possession of your own mind. Self-discipline starts with a mastery of our thoughts. If we do not control our thoughts, we cannot control our deeds. Think first and act afterward. Most people do exactly the reverse of this, that is, act first and think later. The two recipes accompanying this principle require self-discipline when going back for seconds. The Pineapple Upside-Down Cake is an easy recipe that has stood the test of time, and the Apple Dumpling Recipe requires a little more work, but as in all good things the investment of time is worth it. Enjoy.

- Judith Williamson

Pineapple Upside-Down Cake

1 pkg. yellow cake mix

½ c. butter or margarine

1 c. brown sugar

1 (1 lb. 3 oz.) can pineapple slices

drained maraschino cherries

whipped cream

Preheat over to 350 degrees. Melt butter in a 13x9x2 inch pan. Sprinkle brown sugar evenly in pan. Arrange drained pineapple slices and maraschino cherries on top of the sugar mixture.

Mix cake as directed on the label with 1 and 1/3 cups water and 2 eggs. Do not substitute fruit juice for water. Beat as directed.

Pour batter over fruit. Bake at 350 degrees for about 50 minutes or until cake tests done with a toothpick. Let stand 5 minutes for topping to begin to set. Then turn upside down onto a large platter or a cookie sheet. Tap lightly and allow to drain for two to three minutes. Serve warm with whipped cream.

Note: Nobody refuses a piece of this tropical cake.

Apple Dumplings

Apples: 6 tart, firm apples

Dough:

1 ½ c. flour

½ tsp. salt

½ c. margarine or butter

4 ½ T. water

Filling:

¼ stick of butter

½ cup of brown sugar

2 tsp. cinnamon

pinch of nutmeg

ground walnuts or pecans, if desired

raisins, if desired

Mix above dough ingredients as for pie crust. Roll out and cut into six 6 inch squares. Place an apple which has been peeled and cored in the center of each square.

Cream together a ¼ stick of butter, ½ cup of brown sugar, two teaspoons of cinnamon, a pinch of nutmeg, and ground walnuts or pecans, if desired. Place 1 tablespoon of the mixture inside the cored apple. Fold corners of dough over apples and place in a baking pan.

Syrup:

½ c. water

½ c. sugar

½ stick butter

Heat syrup and pour over apples. Bake 35-40 minutes at 425 degrees until apples are golden brown.

Note: This recipe takes some time to prepare but the aroma and the finished product are well worth the effort. Recipe can easily be doubled too. Once you taste these, you will never be satisfied with store bought ones again. Cook up a memory. Make this treat.

Self-Discipline

> " ...means taking possession of your own mind. "
> -Napoleon Hill

Recipe for Fighting Pessimism

You can fight pessimism through complete belief in two of the most basic truths of the Science of Success:

1. "Whatever the mind can conceive and believe, the mind can achieve."
2. "Every adversity and defeat carries the seed of an equivalent benefit, if we are ingenious enough to find it."

Ingredients for Personal Power

Personal power is acquired through a combination of individual traits and habits, some of which will be explained in greater detail as we come to the other sixteen principles of achievement. Briefly, the ten qualities of personal power (which we call the ten-point rule of personal power) are these:

The habit of definiteness of purpose

Promptness of decision

Soundness of character (intentional honesty)

Strict discipline over one's emotions

Obsessional desire to render useful service

Thorough knowledge of one's occupation

Tolerance on all subjects

Loyalty to one's personal associates and faith in a Supreme Being

Enduring thirst for knowledge

Alertness of imagination

You will observe that this ten-point rule embraces only the traits which anyone may develop. You will observe, also, that these traits lead to the development of a form of personal power which can be used without "violating the rights of others." That is the only form of personal power anyone can afford to wield.

To Grow Daily

It doesn't matter how small you were when you first came into this world. What matters is how much you grow each day of your life. It takes great self-discipline to act each day in a way that allows you to grow spiritually, intellectually, economically, and socially. Here are some ways to grow in each of these areas.

Spiritually: Give advice, be humble, correct wrongdoing, forgive, console, tolerate, pray, love your family and friends, and give thanks for all the blessings bestowed on you each day of your life. To have faith is a gift.

Intellectually: Read, write, learn, teach, listen, think, study, and at night go over the events of the day and make notes of your accomplishments. Knowledge is a gift.

Economically: Work, save, invest, economize, do not waste anything, learn to spend less than what you earn, teach your loved ones and others to save. Always remember that how much you save matters more than how much you earn. Utilize your time effectively. Your time is worth more than gold.

Socially: Volunteer in activities to help others, do favors, keep your surroundings clean, plant a tree, donate blood at least once a year (this will also force you to keep yourself healthy). Be there for your friends in good times and bad.

If you keep looking, you will find infinite actions that will help you grow as a person, but you must discipline yourself to do so every day of your life. If you succeed, the world will be a better place and you will be a better person.

—Virginia C. Ward

Arroz Con Leche (Rice with Milk)

- 1 cup long grain rice
- 1 cup water
- 1 cinnamon stick (2–3 inches)
- 1 cup milk
- 1 can (12 ounces) evaporated milk
- 1 can (10 ounces) condensed milk
- 1 teaspoon vanilla extract
- 1 tablespoon brandy
- 1 cup coconut, chopped pecans, or raisins (optional)

In a strainer, rinse the rice with hot water.

In a medium size pot, boil water with cinnamon stick.

Add rice when the water is boiling. Cook at medium-low heat, stirring occasionally.

When the water is almost evaporated (10 to 15 minutes), add plain milk.

Continue cooking about 10 minutes, stirring occasionally.

Add evaporated milk. Continue cooking about 15 to 20 minutes, stirring frequently.

Add condensed milk and cook another 10 to 15 minutes, stirring constantly.

When liquid is all absorbed, remove from heat. Add vanilla and brandy, then stir. At this time, add coconut, pecans, or raisins if you wish.

Let cool 10 to 15 minutes before serving.

Enjoy the delicious Arroz con Leche. It's a yum-yum dessert!

It's hard to have extra time as a mother of six daughters and five stepchildren, and as a full-time consultant in the sewing industry. As an immigrant from Mexico, I have worked hard to become fluent in English and Spanish, and I have been fortunate to have a successful and fulfilling life. I have learned time is valuable, and it's important to take time out of each day for myself, no matter how hard that may be. I have disciplined myself to act in a way that allows me to grow each day. One of the tools that has helped me with this is **Think and Grow Rich**. *My motto: "A stitch with care will never tear" ("Lo que se cose con amor nunca se descose.")*

Direct Your Thoughts, Control Your Emotions, and Ordain Your Destiny

I was accepted to the United States Merchant Marine Academy in Kings Point, New York. This is the same as attending the United States Naval Academy, the Citadel, and you are entering a branch of the armed services. With less than 13% females in my class, it proved to be very challenging.

At the very beginning, during boot camp, I realized that I would have to direct my thoughts and control my emotions if I planned on graduating. I reminded myself and told myself over and over again that I would succeed. I focused on one day at a time to get me through boot camp, my plebe year, my year at sea, and then finally passing my license exams. No matter how discouraged I would start to get, I would redirect my thoughts to the positive and my final goal of graduating with my degree and licenses.

There were times when I wanted to cry and scream in frustration, but I controlled my emotions and would think positive thoughts to overcome those moments. I set small goals, daily goals to reward myself, to feel positive, and to enjoy a small success every day.

I achieved my goal and ordained my destiny at the end of four years with a degree and a license, and prepared for a rewarding career in the marine industry.

—Cathleen Williamson

Vegetarian Cheesy Lasagna

- 2 jars (14 ounces each) spaghetti sauce
- 1 pound Boca or Morningstar veggie beef crumbles
- 8 ounces lasagna noodles
- 8 ounces soft cream cheese
- 16 ounces cottage cheese
- 16 ounces sour cream
- 1/3 cup parmesan cheese
- 8 ounces mozzarella cheese

Heat sauce and Boca meat, adding your favorite spices to taste (such as minced onion, minced garlic, oregano, crushed red pepper, and black pepper). Allow sauce to cook for about 45 minutes for best flavor.

Cook lasagna noodles as directed on package. Drain well and lay noodles out on paper towels.

In a medium bowl, mix cream cheese, cottage cheese, sour cream, parmesan cheese, and 1/2 of the mozzarella cheese.

In a large lasagna pan, layer enough sauce just to cover the bottom. Place one layer of noodles on the sauce. Spread half the cheese mixture on the noodles.

Repeat layers of sauce, noodles, and cheese.

Top with sauce and remaining mozzarella cheese. Sprinkle additional parmesan cheese on top.

Bake at 350 degrees until sauce bubbles at edges of pan and cheese is browned.

Note: All of the cheeses can be replaced with low fat cheeses and still be just as delicious.

I attended the United States Merchant Marine Academy at Kings Point, New York. There I excelled in basketball and softball, competing for the Division III Championship in 2005. I traveled my sophomore/junior year to ports around the world while earning my degree and graduated in June 2006 with a Bachelor of Science and Business in Intermodal Transportation as well as an unlimited tonnage Third Mate's license. I am currently employed with Blue Chip Hotel and Casino as First Mate. Soon I will be achieving my Captain's license. I love being on the water and look forward to the day when I can buy a boat.

Recipe Notes

Napoleon Hill with *Think and Grow Rich*

10. Accurate Thinking

Accurate Thinking is a priceless asset that cannot be purchased for any amount of money. It cannot be borrowed from others. It must be acquired by each individual through the habit of self-discipline. An accurate thinker does not accept the statements of others as factual, but asks the simple question, "How do you know?" This method determines the accuracy of the information. The two recipes for this principle deliver accurate and consistent results. They are easy to prepare and cost effective. How do I know? Be assured that I know because I have made both of them many times and the results are consistent and delicious!

- Judith Williamson

Tuna Casserole

3 (6 oz.) cans solid white tuna in water, drained

1 (16 oz.) package cooked and drained seashell noodles

2 cans condensed cream of mushroom soup

1 c. shredded Cheddar cheese

½ tsp. salt

1 c. frozen peas

1 small can sliced mushrooms

1 small jar pimentos

25 Ritz crackers, crumbled

Preheat the over to 350 degrees. Mix together the drained tuna, cooked noodles, soup, ½ cup cheese, peas, mushrooms, pimentos, and salt. Pour the mixture into a greased casserole and bake for 30 minutes. Top with the Ritz cracker crumbs and remaining cheese. Return the casserole to the oven only long enough for the cheese topping to melt.

Note: Children love this recipe. And, it's healthy for them too.

Holiday Ham

1 oven cooking bag, turkey size

2 T. flour

8-10 lb. fully cooked ham half, bone in

whole cloves, if desired

1 can pineapple rings, drained, reserve juice

½ c. brown sugar

½ c. pineapple juice, reserved

Maraschino cherries

Preheat over to 325 degrees. Shake flour in oven bag; place in roasting pan at least 2 inches deep. Place ham in bag. With toothpicks, secure pineapple rings on surface of ham. Place maraschino cherries in center of each ring. Mix together brown sugar and pineapple juice. Pour on ham. Stud with cloves, if desired. Close bag with nylon tie. Cut 6 half-inch slits in top of bag. Bake for 2 ½ to 3 hours. Let stand in bag 15 minutes. Remove. Discard juice. Slice and serve.

Note: Cleanup is a breeze and ham is always moist, flavorful and tender.

Accurate Thinking

> " *The accurate thinker separates facts from fiction.* "
> -Napoleon Hill

How to Read a Self-Help Book Accurately

A self-help book is not to be skimmed through the same why that you might read a detective novel. Mortimer J. Adler in *How to Read a Book* urges the reader to follow a definite pattern. Here's an ideal one:

Step A. Read for general content. This is the first reading. It should be a fast reading, to grasp the sweeping flow of thought that the book contains. But take the time to underline the important words and phrases. Write notes in the margins and write down briefly the ideas that flash into your mind as you read. Now this obviously may only be done with a book that you own. But the notations and markings make your book more valuable to you.

Step B. Read for particular emphasis. A second reading is for the purpose of assimilating specific details. You should pay particular attention to see that you understand and really grasp, any new ideas the book presents.

Step C. Read for the future. This third reading is more of a memory feat than it is a reading task. Literally memorize passages that have particular meaning to you. Find ways they can relate to problems that you are currently facing. Test new ideas; try them; discard the useless and imprint the useful indelibly on your habit patterns.

Step D. Read—later—to refresh your memory, and to rekindle your inspiration. There is a famous story about the salesman who is standing up in front of a sales manger saying: "Gimme the old sales talk again, I'm getting kinda discouraged." We should re-read the best of our books at such times to rekindle the fires that got us going in the first place.

Accurate Thinking is Critical for Success

When I became computer savvy, one of the first things I did was Google "Napoleon Hill." I was a firm believer in his philosophies of success. My search led me to the Napoleon Hill Foundation web site and the World Learning Center. I called Judy Williamson and introduced myself. Next thing I knew, I was taking the online Success Through PMA course. Judy and I became friends and remain so today. I am one of the original members of the online Mastermind Club.

For me, Napoleon Hill's 17 Principles—especially as set forth in **Law of Success** and **Think and Grow Rich**—are all any positive, forward thinking person needs to be successful. The key, of course, is applying them in your daily life. Unlike much of the personal growth and wealth-building literature, CDs, and seminars out in the market place today, Dr. Hill's work has a purity and authenticity that sets it apart. It is timeless. His works were written to deliver a philosophy to the listener, not to make a buck for the speaker.

In 2004, I began interviewing a cross-section of individuals who have applied Dr. Hill's philosophy to achieve success in their personal and professional lives. These interviews are posted for the online Mastermind Club. My favorite question for my subjects is which of the 17 Principles is most important. The guests have been unanimous that there is no first among equals in the 17 Principles, yet everyone has a principle which—at least for that day—stands a little taller than the others. The principle I gravitate to is Accurate Thinking. For me, having a clear understanding of the facts and how they relate to and impact the resolution of any challenge or opportunity is critical to success.

—RICHARD BANTA

Brilliant Tacos

- 1 pound lean ground beef
- 1 large, fresh, organic tomato
- 1 head Romaine or red leaf lettuce
  extra sharp cheddar cheese
- 1 fresh jalapeño, the bigger and hotter the better, diced
- 1 medium white onion, diced
  salsa (I like one called "Religious Experience")
- 1 packet taco seasoning
  red chile flakes or cayenne pepper
- 1 box taco shells

Preparing this delicious meal is simple. I don't believe in measuring cups, spoons or other crippling instruments to culinary brilliance. Trust your intuition. Always. In everything. 100% of the time.

Preheat oven to 350 degrees.

Brown ground beef in a skillet, then add onion and jalapeño. I like the onion and jalapeño a tad al dente, not quite translucent. Add the taco seasoning and chile flakes or cayenne pepper and simmer.

While meat is cooking, dice the tomato, chop the lettuce, and grate the cheese.

Pop the taco shells in the oven on a cookie sheet for 3 or 4 minutes to warm them up.

When the shells are warm and the meat is done, you are ready to go. Either stuff the ingredients into individual taco shells and cover with the cheese, lettuce, tomato and salsa, or crush the shells on a plate and do the same. The key here is to be bold and brave. Use a little creative vision to create the perfect Brilliant Taco meal.

I am an entrepreneur, attorney, and wealth and mastermind coach. As I turned 50, I found myself rapidly falling behind in technology. Up until then, I believed the best use for a computer was as a doorstop. At 52, accurate thinking helped me realize it was time to overcome my fear of these machines that were clearly going to govern success in the 21st century. I wanted to get a good feeling for what a computer could do and how it might facilitate success. I enrolled in a 90-day program with the goal of becoming computer literate. I achieved this goal, and now I firmly believe the best machine (with a few exceptions) for a doorstop is a television.

Recipe Notes:

"A positive mind finds a way it can be done. A negative mind looks for all the ways it can't be done."

11. Controlled Attention

Controlled Attention is the act of coordinating all the faculties of the mind and directing their combined power to a given end. It is the highest form of self-discipline. Through the application of self-discipline, the factors of definiteness of purpose, imagination, desire, faith, willpower, and the subconscious mind come into play. **Controlled Attention** requires that you make a start and keep on going in a positive mental attitude.

The Classic Pot Roast recipe and the Meat Loaf Recipe allow you to get a head start on dinner when preparation time is short. Both the pot roast and the meat loaf can be prepared in advance, refrigerated overnight, and then popped into the oven to be ready in time for guests. This controlled attention allows you to have time for cleanup and decorating details that otherwise might be delayed due to more demanding recipes. With these two recipes in your back pocket you will be sporting a free and easy attitude at dinnertime.

- Judith Williamson

Classic Pot Roast

1 5-6 lb. chuck pot roast
7-8 whole potatoes, peeled
7-8 stalks of celery, halved
10 carrots, cleaned and halved
10 small to medium onions, peeled
5-6 parsnips, optional
2-3 T. chopped, fresh parsley
2-3 cloves minced garlic
2 packets Pot Roast seasoning (I like Lawry's)
2 cups of water
salt and pepper to taste
1 large cooking bag
2 T. flour

Place two tablespoons flour inside the large oven cooking bag and shake to distribute the flour. Position the bag inside a roasting pan with sides. Place the pot roast inside the bag. Season with salt and pepper. Add the peeled potatoes, onions, celery, carrots, parsnips (optional), chopped parsley, and minced garlic. Prepare the pot roast seasoning as directed with two cups of water and the seasoning packets. Mix, and pour on top of pot roast. Close the bag and secure with tie. Punch six slits on the top of the bag for steam to escape. Bake at 350 degrees for three hours. When done, slit the bag and remove the roast and vegetables to a serving platter. Serve the gravy separately.

Note: This is always a hit with the men in the family.

Meat Loaf

1 lb. ground beef
½ lb. sausage
¼ lb. ground veal
1 c. fresh bread crumbs
1 medium onion, chopped
¾ can Hunt's Tomato Sauce
1 egg, beaten
1 ½ tsp. salt
¼ tsp. pepper

Mix together lightly and form into loaf. Place in shallow pan large enough so that the juices and sauce won't spill over. Place in 350 degree oven while you make the sauce.

Sauce for Meat Loaf

2 T. prepared mustard
2 T. brown sugar
2 T. vinegar
¼ c. tomato sauce
¾ c. water

Mix well and pour over meat loaf, return to oven, bake 1 ¼ hours (more if needed). Skim off grease and serve.

Note: Easy recipe that can even accommodate dinner guests.

Controlled Attention

> " ...leads to mastery in any type of human endeavor. . . . "
> -Napoleon Hill

Supercharged Success Formula in Action!

Here's how to use your knowledge:

1. Concentrate on one principle for an entire week, every day of the week. Respond by proper action every time an occasion arises.

2. And then, start the second week on the second principle or virtue. Let the first be taken over by your subconscious mind. Should an occasion arise when the employment of a previous principle flashes into your conscious mind, use the self-starter DO IT NOW! and then ACT! Continue to concentrate on one principle at a time each week and leave the others to be executed by the habits established in your subconscious as the occasion arises.

3. When the series is completed, start over again. Thus at the end of a year, you will have completed the entire cycle four times.

4. When you have acquired a desired characteristic, substitute a new principle for a new virtue, attitude, or activity that you may wish to develop.

Microwave Recipes!

Let these single ingredient self-motivators give you instant nourishment!

God is always a good God!

Day by day, in every way, through the grace of God, you are getting better and better!

Have the courage to face the truth!

What the mind can conceive and believe, the mind can achieve!

Every adversity has the seed of a greater benefit!

You can do it if you believe you can!

Persistence Pays Off

Ever since birth I have only had sight in one eye, which caused many challenges in my childhood. I had problems playing sports such as baseball, cricket, hockey, and basketball—any sport that involved a moving object. Why? I do not have any depth perception or the ability to see three dimensionally.

As a child I was bullied by classmates because I was not very good at sports. Even worse, many of my teachers would tell my parents that I was stupid and should be put into a slow learner's class. Due to problems at birth there was some damage to the brain which limited my attention span and ability to use long-term memory.

I have endured much pain both physically and emotionally. In the last several years I have had five major eye operations; two doctors have thrown their hands in the air in disgust and quit because the first four operations were failures. The sole doctor left on the team told me that if I was willing to persist and endure the pain, he would stick with me.

Operation number five was a success. Amazing how persistence pays off.

—BOYD MCCLEAN

I know that throughout life we are going to face challenges. Regardless of what they may be, we must keep a positive mental attitude and persist. Without persistence, we are surrendering to mediocrity.

Toffee

- ½ lb. butter
- 1 c. sugar
- 1 T. water
- 1 tsp. vanilla
- ½ c. chopped nuts, if desired
- ½ Hershey chocolate bar
- 3 T. nuts, finely chopped

Place butter, sugar and water in a heavy saucepan. Cook at a rolling boil for ten minutes, until mixture turns a rich brown, stirring constantly. Remove from heat and add vanilla and nuts. Pour into a 9x9 inch pan.

Place ½ Hershey bar on top of hot mass. When softened, spread and sprinkle nuts on top. If desired, mark candy before it hardens.

English Toffee

- 1 c. sliced almonds
- 1 c. butter
- 1 c. granulated sugar
- 1/3 c. dark brown sugar (packed)
- 2 T. water
- 1 T. baking soda
- 2 c. semi-sweet chocolate chips

Sprinkle almonds in a buttered 13x9 inch pan. In large heavy saucepan melt butter; add sugars and water; mix well. Stir constantly. Place thermometer in mix and boil to 300 degrees (hard crack stage). Remove from heat, stir in soda. Work quickly, carefully pour over almonds in pan. Sprinkle chocolate chips over top of toffee and spread evenly as it melts. Chill in refrigerator at least 1 hour. Break into pieces, Makes 1-½ pounds.

Note: A special treat at holiday time for serving and for giving.

Keep Your Mind on the Things You Want and Off the Things You Don't

Often situations arise that get a little voice in my head chattering away. I understand that little voice represents the part of me that is comfortable at a certain spot in my personal growth. As I attempt to reach the next echelon, my survival instinct kicks in and reminds me that I am comfortable now without expanding my horizons. My comfort zone is a place that I am used to, a place that is safe. It is also a place I will not grow from unless I choose to ignore the voice and say, "Thanks for sharing!"

The little voice, the device we all have that keeps us in our "comfort zone," is simply designed and concerned for our survival. It wants to be (and truly is) our friend and protector. It wants to keep us safe from hurt, disappointment, rejection, and failure. It is necessary for us to endure daily life. It does not want us to take chances. It reminds us not to put a hand in the fire or step off the curb in front of a car. If not kept under control and monitored, though, nothing can be more powerful in preventing us from being the best we can be.

I have turned the little voice into a different type of friend. The little voice has become a challenger. Not a nemesis or an opponent, but a friend who allows me to recognize opportunity. When faced with any given situation, we are forced to make choices. My choice is to question the little voice, to heed its concern as I understand its purpose. It is my job to recognize the voice and its intention, then say, "thanks for sharing," and make the appropriate decision for long-term growth.

—Gary Freireich

German Potato Salad

4 slices bacon

1 T. flour

1 T. sugar

½ tsp. salt

½ tsp. dry mustard

½ tsp. celery seed

½ c. water

¼ c. vinegar

6 hard-cooked eggs, sliced

5 medium potatoes, cooked, peeled and chopped

¼ c. chopped green onions with tops celery leaves, optional garnish

In a large skillet over medium heat, cook bacon until crisp. Remove from pan, drain, crumble and set aside. Pour off all but 1 tablespoon bacon drippings. Blend in flour, sugar, salt, mustard and celery seed. Cook, stirring constantly, until mixture is smooth and bubbly. Combine water and vinegar. Stir into flour mixture all at once. Cook until mixture boils and is smooth and thickened.

Reserve 2 center egg slices for garnish. Chop remaining eggs. Add chopped eggs, potatoes, onions and reserved bacon to sauce. Gently stir to mix. Heat to serving temperature. Garnish with reserved egg slices and celery leaves, if desired.

I was born in Chicago, Illinois, in 1955. From early on I had an affinity for understanding how things worked. This evolved into dissecting everything I got my hands on. My interests led me to gravitate towards mechanics, and I went from cars and motorcycles to aircraft. When my children were born, it became necessary to make real money. I chose to pursue home remodeling, because it seemed to provide a good income as well as allowing me to work for myself while learning to build and operate a successful business. Currently, I assist others in building their wealth streams and ultimately realizing their own dreams.

Recipe Notes

W. Clement Stone with Napoleon Hill

12. Teamwork

Teamwork is friendly cooperation with others and it always pays off. When engaged with a positive mental attitude, the result is always a steppingstone to other opportunities. Willing coordination of effort among individuals is a good definition of teamwork. The chicken salad recipe below is one of my favorites. It was shared with me by a team member whom I worked with in an administrative office. When time was short, and lunch was a priority, Juanita would mix up a batch of this the night before and deliver the best-ever lunch to our team. Not only did it inspire us to continue working, but it brought us together as a team. With that in mind, I believe that the Hobo Recipe would be a good one to make at home with children since it would give them an opportunity to share in the cooking and enjoy the results as well. Children could both read and assemble the recipe with adult supervision. These crossover skills are a great way to teach experientially.

- Judith Williamson

Juanita's Special Chicken Salad

3 c. cooked, chopped chicken breasts

1 c. toasted pecan pieces

1 c. green seedless grapes sliced in half

1 c. chopped celery

½ c. mayonnaise or salad dressing

1 T. fresh lemon juice

In a large bowl, mix together the chopped chicken, pecans, grapes, celery, mayonnaise or salad dressing, and lemon juice. Refrigerate two to three hours before serving.

Note: A very tasty and elegant chicken salad.

Hobo Dinner

1 lb. ground round steak

2 tomatoes

2 medium potatoes

1 pkg. frozen and mixed vegetables

1 large onion

1 can mushrooms (6-8 oz.)

salt, pepper, thyme

Salt and pepper ground round, divide into 4 patties. Lightly brown patties in a buttered pan. Do not cook through. Save pan drippings. Place each patty in the center of an 18 inch square of aluminum foil. Top each with ¼ inch thick slices of onion, potato, and tomato. Add ¼ of frozen, mixed vegetables and ¼ of mushrooms to each packet. Season to taste, pour pan drippings on top, and seal, allowing air space for expansion. Bake 1 ½ hours at 350 degrees. Vegetables may be varied to suit individual taste.

Teamwork

> "...harmonious cooperation that is willing and voluntary and free."
> -Napoleon Hill

A Recipe for Teamwork

Team work in a spirit of friendliness costs so little in the way of time and effort, and it pays such huge dividends not only in money, but in the finer things of life. One wonders why so many people go out of their way to make life miserable for themselves and others by failure to recognize this truth. A kindly word here, a kindly deed there, a pleasant smile everywhere, and this world would be a better place for all mankind.

This is the spirit which lights the path to Happy Valley for all who adopt it. And it is the spirit which leads to the attainment of the twelve riches of life:

- a positive mental attitude
- sound physical health
- harmony in human relationships
- freedom from fear
- the hope of achievement
- the capacity for faith
- a willingness to share one's blessings
- a labor of love
- an open mind on all subjects
- self-discipline
- the capacity to understand people
- economic security

What an array of riches, and each of them tied in with that little phrase teamwork!

Teamwork is beneficial because it:

- Inspires every individual connected with the organization with a Definite Major Purpose: a deeply seated desire to contribute to the organization's success.

- Develops self-reliance through self-expression that is free from all fears.

- Encourages the development of the spirit of clean sportsmanship inside and outside of the business.

- Develops leadership by encouraging the exercise of personal initiative and willingness to assume personal responsibility.

- Inspires Teamwork between employees and management, eliminating entirely the usual tendency of people to "pass the buck" and dodge individual responsibility.

- Develops an alert mind and a keen imagination.

- Provides an adequate outlet for the expression of individual ambition on a basis that is highly beneficial to each individual associated with the company.

- Gives everyone a feeling that he or she "belongs" and no one is left without the means of gaining personal recognition on merit.

- Inspires loyalty among the employees, loyalty to the company, and loyalty to one another; thus labor troubles are an unknown circumstance.

- Gives the company the fullest possible benefit of all talents, ingenuity, and Creative Vision of every employee, and provides adequate compensation for these talents in proportion to their value.

Teamwork produces power, but whether the power is temporary or permanent depends upon the motive that inspired the cooperation. If the motive is one that inspires people to cooperate willingly, the power produced by this sort of Teamwork will endure as long as that spirit of willingness prevails. If the motive is one that forces people to cooperate, by fear or any other negative cause, the power produced will be temporary. Great physical power can be produced by coordination of the efforts of individuals, but the endurance of that power, its quality, scope, and strength are derived from that intangible something known as the "spirit" in which people work together for the attainment of a common end. Where the spirit of Teamwork is willing, voluntary, and free it leads to the attainment of a power that is very great and enduring.

Teamwork differs from the Mastermind Alliance:
1. Teamwork (cooperation) is based on the coordination of effort.
2. The Mastermind principle is based on personal relationships with several people who have your direct purposes and goals in mind.

TEAMWORK

A Family Team

My Chinese mother has so much inner strength, it is indescribable. Today, my mother works 12 to 13 hour days as a supervisor in a Los Angeles clothing factory, and comes home—only to cook dinner for 2 hours, for our family.

I feel so blessed to have a mother that is so driven in raising six children. My father and mother arrived in the USA from Hong Kong when I was just two and a half years old.

I feel a family's success depends on love and teamwork. As I'm about to turn 29, these two qualities are such a huge foundation in helping me with my life.

My mother recently told me why she puts so much energy into these meals. She said, "I know I can't afford to take my kids to travel and see the world like some families can, so cooking is my way to show my kids that I love them."

Napoleon Hill says, "Every person who has been moved by genuine love knows that it leaves enduring traces upon the human heart. The effect of our love endures because love is spiritual in nature."

The fish dish is very symbolic of mother showing me how to "fish" for myself.

—SHERYN MADRANO

Steamed Tilapia

- 1 1/2 pound fresh whole tilapia, gutted and scaled
- 6 thin slices fresh ginger, about 1 inch by 2-1/2 inches each
- 3 green onions, whites chopped into 1 inch pieces, greens julienned
- 3 cups water
- 2 tablespoons corn oil
- 5 tablespoons seasoned soy sauce for seafood

Place fish on a large plate that can withstand cooking heat (steaming).

Place 2 ginger slices inside the fish's mouth and 2 slices inside the stomach. Julienne the last two pieces of ginger.

Put half of the green onion whites on the bottom of the plate and the rest on top of the fish.

Place a medium size steamer pot or wok onto stove, with a steamer stand in the middle. Fill with 3 cups of water. Turn on medium heat. When water comes to a full boil, place the fish on the plate into the steamer, cover, and cook for 8 minutes.

Remove fish and plate carefully, with oven gloves. Use the lid of the pot or wok to cover the fish while draining the excess water from the plate.

Place fish back into the steamer. Pour the soy sauce on top of the fish and steam for another 4 minutes.

In a sauce pan, heat the corn oil and sauté the julienne green onion for about 5 seconds.

Place julienned ginger on top of fish and pour the green onions and oil on top of the fish.

Carefully remove fish from the steamer. Serve with jasmine rice and steamed broccoli.

I am 29 years old and was born in Vietnam. My Chinese mother and Vietnamese father arrived in the United States without being able to speak any English. In 2003, I became a Reiki Master, and today I practice in the Los Angeles area.

My Element of Success

Growing up in a family business taught me many things in life. I remember many weekends, evenings, and summer vacations riding in a truck with dad, loading trucks or helping mom in the office. If we wanted to spend time with mom and dad, it usually involved work. If we wanted to have fun, it usually required teamwork—it got the job done faster and more efficiently, leaving more time with mom and dad. We all worked hard alongside mom and dad while watching the company grow.

Teamwork became an important component in my life. If I wanted to accomplish great feats, I knew I couldn't do it alone. Success requires a vision and it requires surrounding yourself with those who share that vision. Growing up, that network was my parents, my siblings, and our extended family. While pursuing a career in dentistry, I found teamwork was an essential element to effective patient care. When I started teaching, I always told my students I had the best of both worlds: I loved dentistry and I loved teaching it. Napoleon Hill states, "Enthusiasm is contagious and teamwork is the inevitable result." I believe my enthusiasm for what I did moved my students and those around me to strive for success. Today, as a principal, I hope that my enthusiasm and passion for career and technical education drive people to work hard. I also hope that my belief that education is only effective if we all work together as an educational team, drives others to inspire student success.

In every facet of life, teamwork is an essential component to our success. It makes life easier. It gets the job done faster. "Teamwork is sharing a part of what you have, a part that is good, with others," said Napoleon Hill. I firmly believe this is true.

—AUDRA PETERSON

Artichoke Dip

1 (15 ounces) can artichoke hearts in water
2 cups mozzarella cheese
1 cup parmesan cheese
1 cup mayonnaise
1 small can water chestnuts

Preheat oven to 350 degrees.

In a blender, chop the artichokes until smooth. Pour into a mixing bowl.

Add all other ingredients and mix together well.

Pour into a 9-inch square glass baking dish. Bake mixture for 30-35 minutes or until golden brown on top.

Serve with tortilla chips or crackers.

Leadership has always intrigued me, and service to others has always been an innate drive for me. As an educational leader, principal, mother, and wife, I lead many people in many directions. I always strive to do what is in the best interest of kids. This brings me great satisfaction. Working on an educational team provides what is best for my students. Working as a family unit helps drive the success of our team. I think the family network becomes a driving force towards my success as an individual. If I did not have the help of all of those around me, I am not sure I would have the personal successes I have been blessed with.

Recipe Notes:

"You must get busy doing something about going the extra mile."

13. Learning From Adversity And Defeat

Hope can be found in the knowledge that every defeat carries with it the seed of an equivalent or greater benefit. This is the reason that many individuals undertake the study of Dr. Hill's philosophy of success. Knowing that things can and do get better after temporary setbacks is the reason people hold onto hope for a better future. Understanding and utilizing this principle is a positive way to manifest changes for the good in our lives. The recipe for Cowboy Beans falls into this category because originally it was named Funeral Beans. Every time a death happened and a buffet was hosted for the family after the service, these beans showed up. People began to look forward to them, and it seemed a shame to wait for a somber event to serve them. So, by being renamed they can now appear tastefully at many other functions. Just think what a name can do! The Corned Beef Hash recipe is included because it reminds me of my son. Considering myself a good cook, I was taken aback one day when I heard Tim say to a friend, "My mom cooks from scrap!" What he meant to say was, "My mom cooks from scratch." Either way, it can be construed as a compliment because sometimes to make ends meet, we have to use what we have on hand. Tight budgets mean that we just have to be to a bit more creative. Yes, learning from adversity and defeat has its advantages.

- Judith Williamson

Cowboy Beans

½ lb. hamburger or sausage

½ lb. bacon

¾ c. onion, chopped

No. 2 can pork and beans

No. 2 can kidney beans, drained

No. 2 can lima beans, drained

No. 2 can butter beans, drained

½ c. brown sugar

½ c. sugar

1 tsp. salt

½ c. catsup

1 tsp. dry mustard

2 T. vinegar

Brown hamburger and bacon; drain. Add onions and beans. Add brown sugar, white sugar, salt, catsup, dry mustard, and vinegar. Put in casserole dish and bake in 350 oven for 40 minutes.

Note: Instead of baking, this dish can also be cooked in a crock pot.

Corned Beef Hash Patties

Mix together:

15 oz. corned beef hash

½ onion (chopped or grated)

1 egg

Beat well and add:

1 bell pepper, chopped

1 stalk celery, chopped

1 T. self rising corn meal

1 T. grape nuts (if you have them)

Form into patties, dip into flour and fry until brown on both sides.

Note: A good recipe that utilizes things on hand.

Learning from Adversity and Defeat

> " Every adversity carries with it a seed of an equivalent or greater benefit. "
> -Napoleon Hill

Recipe for Getting Rid of Guilt

Is guilt haunting you? Get rid of it once and for all by following this recipe.

... First of all, you listen as you hear advice, a lecture, an inspirational sermon that could change your life.

... Then you count your blessings, and thank God for them. Feel sincerely sorry and ask for forgiveness. When you realize your blessings, it isn't difficult to become sincerely sorry for the wrongs you have done. And truly to repent. Then you will have the courage to ask for forgiveness from God.

... You must take the first step forward. This is important because it is a symbol through a physical gesture that you make in the direction of a changed life.

... Also, you must make amends by taking the second step forward: begin immediately to right every wrong.

... And then the most important step of all: apply the Golden Rule. This should be easy. For now when you are tempted to do wrong, that "still, small voice" will whisper to you. And when it does, stop and listen. Count your blessings. Picture yourself in the other fellow's place. And then make your decision to do what you would want done if you actually were in his position.

Recipe for Life

Life, you can't subdue me, because I refuse to take your discipline seriously.

When you try to hurt me, I laugh, and laughter knows no pain.

I appropriate your joys wherever I find them. Your sorrows neither discourage nor frighten me, for there is laughter in my soul.

When I get the thing I want, I am glad, but temporary defeat does not make me sad. I simply set music to the words of defeat and turn it into a song about laughter.

Your tears are not for me. I like laughter much better, and because I like it, I use it as a substitute for grief and sorrow and pain and disappointment.

Life, you are a fickle trickster, don't deny it!

You slipped the emotion of love into my heart so you might use it as a thorn with which to prick my soul, but I have learned to dodge your trap—with laughter.

You try to lure me with the desire for gold, but I have outwitted you by following the trail which leads to Knowledge, instead.

You induce me to build beautiful friendships; then convert my friends into enemies, so you may harden my heart, but I sidestep your fickleness by laughing off your attempt and selecting new friends in my own way.

You cause men to cheat me in trade, so I will become hard and irritable, but I win again because I possess only one precious asset, and this is something no man can steal—IT IS THE POWER TO THINK MY OWN THOUGHTS AND BE MYSELF, plus the capacity to laugh at you for your pains.

You threaten me with Death, but to me Death is nothing worse than a long, peaceful sleep, and sleep is the sweetest of human experiences except laughter.

You build the fire of Hope in my breast, then sprinkle water on the flames, but I go you one better by rekindling the fire on my own account—and laugh at you once more.

You plant vicious enemies in my path who try to assault my reputation and destroy my self-reliance, but you fail again because I turn their efforts into publicity which brings me to the attention of new friends whom I would never know without this perfidy.

For a quarter of a century, you hurdle-jumped me over every conceivable form of failure, but I coined the knowledge gained from these failures into a philosophy of Success which now renders useful service and brings countless thousands of others the joy of laughter; and these newly made friends willingly pay me compound interest for every second of failure you have imposed upon me.

You bore me into this world in poverty, but this has proved to be a blessing in disguise because poverty has taught me patience and industry and imagination and temperance and humility and a hundred other useful traits which the idle will never know.

Life, you are licked as far as I am concerned, because you have nothing with which to lure me away from laughter and you are powerless to scare me.

LEARNING FROM ADVERSITY AND DEFEAT

The Turning Point

Through a series of events that Napoleon Hill terms "adversity and defeat," I lost my marketing and communications firm. What had been taken away was about to be replaced with something better.

I had a client who believed in me and she asked me to join her team at the Rock Island Housing Authority (RIHA), which provides housing assistance to low-income families, elderly, and disabled persons. It receives most of its funding through the U. S. Department of Housing and Urban Development. I became immersed in the challenges associated with working for a federally funded entity. I also became familiar with the obstacles facing the clientele the organization serves, many of whom are third and fourth generation welfare recipients.

One day, I received **Napoleon Hill's Magic Ladder to Success**. In the back of the book there is a list of the 30 most common causes of failure. Number one is "Unfavorable Hereditary Foundation," the social construct or environment in which one is born and raised, e.g., welfare. It was then that I discovered my definite purpose: I had to get these concepts into the hands of the children and break the welfare cycle!

I contacted the Napoleon Hill Foundation and spoke to Judy Williamson. She said if I could gain the support of RIHA, she would develop the program and train the trainers. RIHA also hired a consultant to teach us how to research, identify, and solicit private foundations for the funding of worthwhile projects. As part of the hands-on training, I used my newfound purpose as my topic for research. The seeds of equivalent benefit have begun to germinate and produce magnificent results.

—GAIL BROOKS

Chocolate Chip Cake

1-1/4 cup boiling water
1 cup dates
1 teaspoon baking soda
3/4 cup shortening
1 cup sugar
2 eggs
1/2 teaspoon vanilla
2 cups of flour
4 tablespoons cocoa
1/4 teaspoon salt
1 package (16 ounces) chocolate chips
1/4 cup sugar
1/2 cup walnuts or pecans, chopped

Preheat oven to 350 degrees.

In a small bowl, pour boiling water over dates and baking soda. Let stand until cool.

Cream shortening and sugar together. Add eggs and vanilla and beat well. Fold date mixture in to form batter.

In a separate bowl, mix flour, cocoa, and salt. Add dry ingredients to batter.

Spread batter into a 9-inch by 13-inch baking pan. Sprinkle chocolate chips, sugar, and nuts on top of batter.

Bake at 350 degrees until a skewer or toothpick comes out clean, approximately 16–20 minutes.

I always knew I had a purpose (somewhere). I knew I was created to fulfill a dream—I just couldn't figure out exactly what it was. Oh, I had some hints. I had caught a fleeting glance of it now and again and even had it within my grasp a few times. But I could never seem to pin it down, to wrap my arms around it, to completely identify and articulate it. I had not yet made it "mine." But now that I have reached the age Oprah Winfrey refers to as the "new 30," my focus has become, well, a little more focused. I have a plan!

Planting Seeds of Opportunity

One of the most important lessons in life is that every adversity carries with it the seed of an equivalent or greater benefit. When I left home at a young age, I was uneducated and unemployable. I lived on the streets, by my wits and instinct. After facing these challenges for more than six years, I knew I wanted more out of life.

Education was the first step. I chose a definite major purpose to complete college and develop a career. I moved across the country, took the GED test, and passed despite my sixth-grade education. Soon I was enrolled in a nursing certificate program at a community college. I didn't have any of the skills needed to complete a college course, no organization, no note-taking, no study habits, only a burning desire to become a nurse. I tape-recorded every lecture and transcribed each one at home, studying from those verbatim notes.

Although I knew nothing of Napoleon Hill and the Principles of Success, I was using many of them: applied faith, personal initiative, creative vision, controlled attention, accurate thinking, and budgeting time and money, to name a few. As I look back now, a registered nurse certified for critical care, I realize that from the adversity and despair of life as a lost child on the streets, the seed of benefit grew in me, building my confidence and self-reliance to the point I could take the first steps toward becoming a nurse and eventually an advocate for women and children at risk.

—LAURA DIETRICH-LAKE

Mango Pineapple Salsa

Spicy but sweet, just like life!

- 1 medium red onion, finely chopped
- 1-2 jalapeños, finely minced
- 3 large ripe mangos, peeled and diced
- 1 can (12 ounces) crushed pineapple, drained
- 1 bunch (3/4 cup) fresh cilantro, minced
- 2 limes, juiced
- 1 pinch salt

This recipe is best made with a salsa maker, but also can be made by hand with excellent results. Food processors are not recommended.

Peel the onions and rough chop. Add to salsa maker.

Cut jalapeños in half and de-vein. Remove all seeds. (For hotter salsa, leave seeds in to taste.) Add jalapeño halves to salsa maker.

Close lid and crank salsa maker until there is a fine, uniform dice. Do not over-work until liquid forms. (This tends to occur in regular food processors and will ruin your salsa.) Remove onion and pepper mixture to a large mixing bowl.

Peel mangos and rough chop into 2" cubes. Add to salsa maker and crank a few times, just enough to break them down slightly. Add to mixing bowl. Drain pineapple thoroughly and add to mixing bowl.

Mince fresh cilantro by hand. Never use dried herbs in this recipe, they will overpower the flavors. Add cilantro to mixing bowl.

Juice two limes into mixing bowl, being careful of any seeds. Mix thoroughly. Add salt to taste.

May be served immediately or refrigerated (covered) for several hours to enhance the flavors. Overnight is ideal.

From a career healing those with injury and disease, I know all too well how life can be unbalanced. So many of us equate healing with doctors and hospitals, not realizing we have the power within us to change our realities. Self-healing is available to all of us at any time; we simply have to have faith and act.

LEARNING FROM ADVERSITY AND DEFEAT

Learning from Adversity and Defeat Brings Many Blessings

I am a beginner at learning and applying Napoleon Hill's Science of Success. For 35 years I have continually battled with my physical challenge of being very overweight. I have applied almost every method known to man trying to overcome this giant on my heels. I have had many successes that later turned into failures. I am sure there are many of you who know what that feels like.

I was just about to give up on this long, difficult journey when I was lovingly told about this wonderful man named Napoleon Hill who developed a philosophy comprising 17 principles by interviewing over 500 famous men and women. He asked them what actions they applied every day to their lives that made them successful.

The success principle I love most is "learning from adversity and defeat." This principle has taught me that I am not a failure after all; I am so much stronger than I give myself credit for, because I have continued applying many strategies over a 35-year period. I have learned many things through all the books I've read and programs I have tried. I am grateful for that knowledge. I also learned that you have only failed when you give up entirely. Through my renewed weight loss efforts, I am blessed each day with improving health. My asthma doesn't bother me anymore. I can walk up stairs more easily, and it feels great to move more.

I realize even more now how sacred our gift of life is, and that we must always fight to preserve it. I also realize that the adversary wants nothing more than to see us all miserable and willing to lie down and surrender. I am never giving up!

—DEBRA T. WATKINS

Lemon Basil Halibut

A healthful and elegant entrée for guests.

    4 halibut steaks (6 ounces each)
    1 teaspoon paprika
    1/2 cup low fat margarine
    1 tablespoon fresh basil, finely minced
    1 tablespoon lemon juice
    1 tablespoon green onion, finely minced
       nonfat cooking spray

Lightly coat the grill with cooking spray and preheat for 5 minutes.

Place steaks on the grill and sprinkle with paprika. Grill for 6-8 minutes or until fish flakes easily.

In a small bowl, blend margarine, basil, lemon juice, and green onion.

To serve, arrange each steak on a plate and top with a generous spoonful of the lemon-basil butter.

I want to express my gratitude to those who are always willing to share their new discoveries with me. Remember to go out there and open your mouth about these wonderful principles, for I was once a person ready to give up after 35 years of trying.

Adversity is Like an Onion

When the taste of a newly picked onion is first encountered, it is strong, bitter and disagreeable. But given the blending of other foods and seasonings, the onion's flavor becomes very pleasing.

When my husband died, my life was like a newly picked onion. I had a young daughter to finish raising. I did not think I would endure.

Three months after my husband's death, I began a new job, dove into a new career, and hoped for the best.

Then I encountered another roadblock, and two months into the job, I reached a new low in my life. There were so many problems affecting the agency where I worked, the obstacles seemed insurmountable. The company's very existence was at stake. I felt I wasn't capable of taking the agency beyond its problems.

But failure was not an option.

I formed a mastermind alliance. Help came from everywhere. In the beginning, change was very gradual. But then the positive changes came by leaps and bounds.

Today my daughter is grown, living on her own and doing well. The agency is a success and looking at expansion.

Life is a joy to be shared and passed on.

—LISA WEIN

Barley and Mushroom Casserole

2 ounces dried mushrooms
2 cups water
1 box medium barley
2 sticks butter
2 cloves garlic, crushed

Soak dried mushrooms in 2 cups water overnight, then drain.

Boil barley for 50 minutes as indicated on box. Drain.

Preheat oven to 325 degrees.

Melt butter with the garlic. When the butter has melted, mix in barley and mushrooms.

Place mixture in a 9-inch square baking dish. Cover with foil and bake for 30–40 minutes. Remove foil, increase temperature to 375 degrees, and bake uncovered for 10 more minutes, until golden brown.

I am Director of Haven House, a safe-haven for victims of domestic violence and/or abuse. I provide shelter, food, clothing, and educational programs for women in need of these services.

LEARNING FROM ADVERSITY AND DEFEAT

Never, Never, Never, Never, Never, Never Give Up!

This phrase has always been my motivating force, as a kid growing up, and through my many challenges, failures, setbacks, and successes. I believe adversity and defeat challenge us more than anything else in life. More than competitions in sports and other events, more than winning over the heart of the special person that has caught our eye, more than the demands of a job.

Adversity and defeat are like growing pains because as we experience them and overcome them, as Napoleon Hill teaches, there is always a seed of an equivalent or greater benefit. This is easy to say and much harder to believe when we are actually experiencing the problems day after day. It sometimes overwhelms us, creating a cloud of negative thoughts and depression that engulf us.

Equally as real, as long as we don't give in, give up, and accept the despair, is the light at the end of the tunnel—which may only be a glimmer. We have to hold on to that and have faith in our God, our Heavenly Father, that He desires our success as much or more than we do.

The adversities we go through are for our own good. They teach us and give us experience that will help us or help us help others. That is looking at the big picture of life. Sometimes we can only see the little picture of the moment we are in, yet deep down we have to hold on to hope and faith that the moment is brief and it will get better. When we look around we can always find someone else worse off than we are. I can write this from my own experience: adversity and defeat is not failure unless we accept it as such.

—ALLEN WATKINS

Hershey's Chocolate Barbecue Sauce

1/2 cup olive oil
1/4 cup garlic, chopped
2 cups onion, diced
4 whole lemons, juiced
2 tablespoons salt
3 tablespoons black pepper
2 tablespoons paprika
2 tablespoons hot pepper sauce
8 cups ketchup
1 cup cider vinegar
4 cups Hershey's chocolate syrup

In a 5 quart sauce pot, heat oil and add garlic and onion. Cook over medium heat until onions are tender.

Add lemon juice, salt, pepper, paprika, and hot sauce. Simmer for 10 minutes.

Add ketchup, vinegar, and chocolate syrup. Simmer for another 15 minutes, and the sauce is ready to slather on your favorite barbecued meat.

I am a real estate investor, broker, REO specialist, business owner, author, and national speaker. Since graduating from the "College of Hard Knocks," I have bought, owned, and sold millions of dollars worth of real estate. Adversity and defeat did not hold me back, and I spend a significant amount of my time helping others find their way to success. In my free hours, I enjoy spending time with my wife and three sons. I am also active in our church, where I am a Home Teacher and Scoutmaster of our Boy Scout troop.

Recipe Notes

Napoleon Hill with Thomas Edison

14. Creative Vision

Dr. Hill states that **Creative Vision** is the product of a well-defined purpose and it has at its base the spirit of the universe which expresses itself through us. He adds that **Creative Vision** recognizes no such thing as the regularity of working hours, is not concerned with monetary compensation, and its highest aim is to do the impossible. Wow! What a compliment when someone says that you are creative! Taking all of the above into account, if you are creative, that makes you nothing short of a miracle worker!

Creativity demands respect. When the creator – little "c" – begins to work on a project, the rest of us must stand aside and let the Creator – big "C" – do the work through the individual doing the project, or even ourselves if we are the creator. Cooking involves creativity. Not just in the preparation of the dish, but in the selection of the recipe, in the creation of the recipe first in our mind, and then in reality. Creativity is work – just not work that is immediately visible. Each of us can be creative – we are hardwired for it from birth – but we may have to experiment to find our best creative medium. Try the two recipes below as expressions of creativity! The Chili and the Tarts allow for fresh expression because you can easily add or subtract what is not pleasing to your personal palette in the recipes. With the nut tarts I sometimes substitute jams and jellies for the nut filling, and the recipe works equally well.

- Judith Williamson

Cincinnati 5-Way Chili

1 lb. finely ground round steak
2 medium onions minced
2 cloves garlic, minced
1 c. tomato sauce
2 T. catsup
1 c. water
1 T. red wine vinegar
1 T. chili powder
1 T. paprika
1 tsp. pepper
1 tsp. honey
½ oz. unsweetened chocolate, grated
½ tsp. each ground cumin, tumeric
½ tsp. each marjoram, allspice
½ tsp. cinnamon
¼ tsp. nutmeg, ground cloves
¼ tsp. mace, ground coriander
¼ tsp. ground cardamon
½ bay leaf, crumbled
1 tsp. salt.

Salt a large cast iron skillet. Turn heat to medium and add meat, onions, and garlic. Cook until meat is browned. Add tomato sauce, catsup, water, and vinegar. As mixture begins to boil, add everything else. Adjust spices to suit your taste. Cover and simmer at very low heat for about 1 hour, stirring and tasting occasionally. Add tomato juice if it is getting to dry to ladle over spaghetti.

Serve over cooked spaghetti or other pasta.

Note: A nice version of an Ohio classic.

Nut Tarts

Basic Dough:
1 (8 oz.) pkg. cream cheese
1 c. margarine
2 c. flour

Let margarine and cream cheese soften to room temperature. Combine cream cheese and butter, then blend in flour to form a soft dough. Chill at least 1 hour or overnight.

Shape the dough into 40 walnut-sized balls. Press each ball of dough into cups of an ungreased mini-muffin tin cup.

Filling:
2 eggs
1 c. brown sugar
2 tsp. vanilla
2 T. butter, melted
1¼ c. chopped nuts, walnuts, pecans, etc.

Beat eggs with wooden spoon. Add brown sugar, melted butter, and vanilla. Mix well. Stir in nuts. Fill each unbaked tart shell ¾ full. Bake at 350 degrees, 25-30 minutes. Cool in pan before removing. Dust tops with powdered sugar when cool. Makes forty tarts.

Note: Use a tart shaper dipped in flour to shape perfect tarts. Don't have one? Use the rounded end of a small wooden rolling pin. Works just as well. Remember to dip in flour each time so that the soft dough does not stick to the rolling pin.

Creative Vision

> **"...is developed by the free and fearless use of one's imagination."**
> -Napoleon Hill

Let's Go Idea Shopping!

Ideas are stored in a big warehouse easily accessible by anyone.

Interviewed by Napoleon Hill, Dr. Gates shares his findings on the sources of all ideas. He states that ideas come from:

1. Knowledge stored in the subconscious mind and acquired through individual experience, observation, and education.
2. Knowledge accumulated by others through the same media, which may be communicated by telepathy.
3. The great universal storehouse of Infinite Intelligence, wherein is stored all knowledge and all facts, and which may be contacted through the subconscious section of the mind.

Two Ingredients for Imagination

Synthetic imagination, which consists of a combination of previously recognized ideas, concepts, plans, or facts arranged in a new order, or put to a new use.

Creative imagination, which has its base in the subconscious section of the mind, and serves as the medium by which basically new facts or ideas are revealed through the faculty of the sixth sense.

A Recipe for Creative Vision

Imagination and creative vision work as much to recreate a memory as to formulate a path for the future. Here at the Napoleon Hill World Learning Center we feature a walking meditation using a labyrinth that I create on grass during our annual open house. The labyrinth is a pattern that has been used for thousands of years as a kinesthetic form of meditation. Your body and mind open as you walk a unicursal path.

Taking time out to meditate may just give you a transforming "a-ha!" moment in which everything must change or rearrange to accommodate a vision or inspiration received.

Before starting your meditation time, decide on a focus, a success phrase, a mantra, or a theme you will concentrate upon. There are three basic "ingredients" to keep in mind upon walking the labyrinth (or whenever meditating): Release, Receive, and Return.

Release: Let go of all worries and other distracting thoughts before you begin. Clear your mind. You cannot receive if you have no receptive vessel.

Receive: Be open to receive from infinite intelligence. During your meditation you will receive illumination. Be aware of the creative thoughts coming to you as you meditate.

Return: Return to your world renewed and with a sense of inspired purpose, ready to implement and share revelations received.

If we can for a moment believe man can fly, the possibility of flying becomes more real. Only by taking time out to suspend our disbelief can we manifest the impossible.

—URIEL MARTINEZ
"CHINO"

Ofelia's Mexican Rice

2/3 cup corn oil (approximately)
2 cups rice
2-1/2 cups water
2 chicken bouillon cubes
2 slices yellow onion
1 can (8 ounces) tomato sauce
1/2 teaspoon salt, or to taste

On medium flame, fill 12-inch pan with enough oil that it touches each side of pan walls. Add rice and stir occasionally until rice is slightly browned.

In a sauce pan, mix water, bouillon cubes, and salt. Bring to boil, then reduce to simmer until needed.

When rice is slightly browned, drain oil. Push rice to one side of pan and put onion on the bare spot. Brown very lightly (enjoy the sizzle).

Add tomato sauce to rice and onions (see the puff of smoke). Stir to distribute ingredients.

Add simmering bouillon water and again stir for an even consistency. Make sure the water covers at least 1/8 inch above the rice. Add more water if needed.

Reduce heat and simmer. After 10 minutes check to see if more water is needed. (Don't let it get too dry.)

Rice should be ready in 20 to 25 minutes. You may turn off heat after 20 minutes and let sit for another 5 minutes if necessary.

Meditating is a transforming force. Water turns to vapor with heat. The same molecules are there, only rearranged. Mom passed away December 29th, 2004, but I can still feel her presence when I combine creative imagination and rice.

Sharing this rice recipe is my way of sharing her memory and another way of telling my Mom, "I'll love you forever."

As executive assistant to the Director of the Napoleon Hill World Learning Center, I wear many hats. I have a degree in Graphic Art and Design and I enjoy assisting the Director with programs and seminars for the Learning Center. It was my calling to service-oriented work that brought Judy and I together when we both worked for the bishop of our Catholic diocese. We now perform a wide variety of work as the "purveyors" of Napoleon Hill's 17 Principles of Success, which gives us great job satisfaction. I have had the privilege of designing covers for the more recent publications for Napoleon Hill Foundation, including this cookbook.

Trusting in Your Dreams

I have been a student of Napoleon Hill's wisdom for the past ten years. It works! In Dr. Hill's words, "Creative vision is definitely and closely related to that state of mind known as faith, and it is significant that those who have demonstrated the greatest amount of creative vision are known to be people with a great capacity for faith." Blending your faith in Infinite Intelligence with faith in your importance to the fabric of society will open up a tapestry of color and experiences that is created from the workshop of your mind and soul . . . your imagination.

Creative Vision allows your heart to soar and your mind to capture your dreams in more vivid and specific definition. You can actually imagine yourself being and doing what you love and aspire to be and do. Draw from each of your senses to enrich the vision. Invest time each day to this reverie. Allow yourself to dream big and authentically. Listen to how your heart feels throughout the experiences. Probe yourself as you refine your vision, and begin to plan a time frame. Prioritize the sequence of events that will lead you along this journey to the "end in mind." Learn daily. Remain open for subtle changes. Share your vision with those who embrace these principles of success. Begin a journal and carry it into a plan for implementation. The benefits to applying these principles are endless. Trusting your dreams brings more meaning to each of the days of your life, transforming *you* toward your heart's delight. When your heart is delighted, it is open and warm, allowing your capacity to love and be loved to grow infinitely. Enjoy your mirrors of love as you reflect your best, unfolding each day like a human rose in bloom.

—CHERI LUTTON

Shrimp Pasta Primavera

- 8 ounces fettuccine, cooked and drained
- 1 1/2 tablespoons olive oil
- 4 cloves garlic, minced
- 16 ounces raw shrimp, peeled, deveined, tails removed
- 1 green bell pepper, sliced
- 1 yellow sweet pepper, sliced
- 1 red sweet pepper, sliced
- 8 ounces fresh mushrooms, sliced
- 1/2 teaspoon black pepper
- 1 pinch salt
- 2 tablespoons fresh basil, chopped
- 1 tablespoons fresh oregano, chopped
- 2 tablespoons butter or margarine
- 1 cup whole milk
- 1/2 cup plus 1 teaspoon parmesan cheese, grated
- 1/4 teaspoon nutmeg

Heat 1/2 tablespoon oil in a large skillet at medium heat. Stir in garlic and cook uncovered for 30 seconds. Add shrimp and stir mixture, cooking uncovered for 3 minutes or until shrimp are opaque. Add remaining oil and stir to coat evenly. Add sliced peppers and mushrooms and stir mixture for 2–3 minutes or until colors are more vibrant and vegetables are slightly tender. Add black pepper, salt, basil, and oregano. Stir thoroughly. Add cooked fettuccine to mixture and toss to coat evenly. Cover and keep warm on simmer heat.

In sauce pan, melt butter at low heat. Add milk, 1/2 cup cheese, and nutmeg. Stir and cook sauce to desired consistency. Place in sauce server for individual servings.

Serve family-style in a large platter, with a splash of the sauce and sprinkled with remaining parmesan cheese. Garnish with sprigs of parsley.

It was New Year's Eve, and I was on a plane heading for London. Although being an international marketing executive was exciting and rewarding, I was teary-eyed. I was leaving my wonderful husband, young daughter, and son behind on a special holiday. There I was, alone; there they were, without me. I prayed for guidance. Instantly, I felt a sense of warmth and unity, and began to understand that my life was on purpose. I realized I had the choice and power to dream the life I desired beyond the present. That flight took me further than Europe. It began my journey of creating the balanced lifestyle that I now enjoy.

Just Imagine

Napoleon Hill wrote that everyone has an imagination. They just don't put it to use. What a shame! Studies show that 90 percent of us are visual. We can only see what is there in front of us. Why is that? Because we do not put our imagination to the test.

In Napoleon Hill's *Magic Ladder of Success*, he writes, "No man ever accomplished anything, ever created anything, ever built any plan or developed a definite chief aim without the use of his or her imagination!"

After marriage, my career as a CPA did not permit me to be the hands-on mother and wife that I wanted to be for my family. I put plans into action to start my own design business whereby I could set my working hours around the needs of my family.

As an interior designer, I have to imagine every day. I have to envision what most of my clients cannot. I take that vision, which might start with a swatch of fabric, a prized piece of art, or grandmother's antique chair, and turn that into a beautiful and welcoming environment.

—DONNA GREEN SIKORSKI

Tilapia with Lemon Vinaigrette

- 5 tablespoons extra virgin olive oil
- 3 shallots, sliced thin
- 1 large head radicchio, coarsely chopped
- 1 can (15 ounces) cannellini beans, drained and rinsed
- 1/3 cup chicken or fish broth
- salt and pepper to taste
- 6 tilapia fillets, about 6 ounces each
- 1/2 cup all purpose flour

Heat 2 tablespoons olive oil in heavy large skillet over medium heat. Add shallots and sauté until tender. Add the radicchio and sauté until wilted, about 5 minutes. Add beans and broth. Cook until heated through. Season with salt and pepper.

Heat 3 tablespoons olive oil in nonstick frying pan over medium high heat. Season fillets with salt and pepper. Dredge the fillets in flour to coat. Shake off excess flour and fry fillets until golden brown and cooked through. Spoon the radicchio mixture over the center of plates. Top with the fillets. Drizzle with lemon vinaigrette.

Lemon Vinaigrette:
- 1/4 cup fresh-squeezed lemon juice
- 1/4 cup Italian parsley
- 2 cloves garlic
- 2 teaspoons finely grated lemon zest
- 1/2 teaspoon salt
- 1/4 teaspoon pepper
- 1/3 cup extra virgin olive oil

Add lemon juice, parsley, garlic, lemon zest, salt, and pepper to a blender. Mix at medium speed. With the machine running, gradually add olive oil. Adjust to taste with salt and pepper.

I have always appreciated art, antiques, and beautiful things. My parents exposed me early on to antique auctions, art galleries, and historical homes. I graduated college with an accounting degree and worked for several years as a Certified Public Accountant before following my passion and becoming an interior designer. I should tell you that my inspirations growing up were a father who always told me that I could do anything that I set my mind to (he just happens to be the Executive Director of the Napoleon Hill Foundation) and the library of Dr. Hill's writings at my fingertips.

Recipe Notes:

"Most illness begins with a negative mind."

15. Maintenance Of Sound Health

The French psychologist, Emil Coué, gave the world a very simple formula for maintaining a sound health consciousness. He recommended the daily repetition of this sentence: "Every day in every respect, I am getting better and better." Once the subconscious mind picks up the message and acts on it, the result is good health. The opposite side of the coin is the statement: "If you think you are sick, you are." Which one do you want to adopt? Our mind cannot hold two thoughts at once. The predominating thought is the one that literally impresses our subconscious mind and brings about the involuntary powerful actions that produce the changes on a cellular level. If we remember the simple phrase, thoughts are things, we know internally that what we think about we become. Keeping this in mind, here's two simple recipes for side dishes as you think about dinner. They're easy and nutritious.

- Judith Williamson

Cole Slaw

2 bags of pre-shredded supermarket cole slaw

1 to 1 and ½ large chopped Vandalia onions

1 green pepper, chopped

2-3 stalks of celery, chopped

1 cup of snipped parsley, loosely packed (use scissors for the snipping!)

1 and ½ cups boiling water

¾ cup sugar

1 cup white or cider vinegar

½ cup canola or vegetable oil

1 tbsp. celery seed

2 tsp. mustard seed

ground salt and pepper to taste

½ chopped red pepper or small jar pimento finely chopped for color, if desired.

1 cup chopped red cabbage, if desired

Combine pre-packaged cole slaw, onions, green pepper, celery, parsley, red pepper or pimento, red cabbage, celery seed, and mustard seed in large glass bowl. Boil water. When boiling, add sugar, vinegar, oil, salt and pepper. Mix well. Pour over cole slaw. Mix well. Cover and refrigerate. Serve with slotted spoon in individual bowls.

Jell-O with Fruit

2 small packages of red Jell-O (3 ounces each) - cherry or raspberry

1 can mandarin oranges

1 can fruit cocktail

1 cup frozen raspberries or blackberries

Boil 2 cups of water. Pour over Jell-O. Mix until completely dissolved. Drain canned fruit. Reserve liquid. Add reserved liquid plus additional amount of cold water to Jell-O to make 2 cups. Mix well. Stir in fruit. Refrigerate until firm – 4 to 5 hours. Serve with whipped cream or plain.

Maintenance of Sound Health

> " Sound health begins with a sound health consciousness. "
> -Napoleon Hill

Recipe for Solitude

I love my family and my friends. My love for them is deep and sincere. I would do anything within my power to add to their comfort and welfare... but, I also love to get away from the crowds, away from everybody, and visit with myself. This may seem rather selfish, but it isn't. My mental development demands it.

I love to think, to look ahead, and anticipate the experiences yet to come in my life, to figure out why I am here and what to do to fulfill my real mission in life. I love to go just a step further in imagination than I have ever gone in realization. In other words, I love to do what many call "dreaming."

Contrary to what some may believe, dreaming is not harmful. In fact, quite the reverse is true. Getting away from others to dream allows you to rise above commonplace thoughts and things.

Milton did his best work after blindness forced him to turn to solitude for realization.

Francis Scott Key wrote the "Star Spangled Banner" while being held as a prisoner of war on a British ship.

When we are with others, we must be polite and discuss with them whatever subject they may happen to bring up. When we are with ourselves, we can direct our thoughts along any line we choose and concentrate upon those thoughts, impress them upon our minds, and keep them where we may get them when we want them.

This is constructive dreaming!

No one ever becomes a "doer" without first becoming a "dreamer." The architect first draws the picture of a building in his mind and then places it on paper. And so we must all see the object of our labors in our minds before we can see them in reality.

Recipe for Mental Equipment

There follows a list of very desirable qualities which almost any normal and reasonable person can come to possess and exercise. The list is long and perfection may be only slowly attained. Therefore, before entering into a detailed consideration of the things you would like to have your mind and body capable of doing, let's at once enumerate those which are absolutely necessary.

1. Physical fitness is of tremendous importance for the simple reason that neither mind nor body can function well without it. Therefore, give attention to your habits of life, proper diet, healthful exercise, and fresh air.

2. Courage must be the part of every man or woman who succeeds in any undertaking, especially that of selling in these trying times of intense competition after a devastating period of depression and discouragement.

3. Imagination is an absolute requisite of a successful salesman. He must anticipate situations and even objections on the part of his prospective customer. He must have such a lively imagination as to enable its operation to place him in sympathetic understanding with the position, needs, and objectives of his customer. He must almost literally stand in the other man's shoes. This takes real imagination.

4. Speech. The tone of voice must be pleasing. A high-pitched squeaky voice is irritating. Words half swallowed are hard to understand. Speak distinctly and enunciate clearly. A meek voice indicates a weak person. A firm, clean-cut, clear voice that moves with assurance and color, indicates an aggressive person with enthusiasm and aggressiveness.

5. Hard work is the only thing that will turn sales training and ability into money. No amount of good health, courage, or imagination is worth a dime unless it is put to work; and the amount of pay a salesman gets is usually fixed by the amount of very hard, intelligent work that he actually puts out. Many people side-step this factor of success.

MAINTENANCE OF SOUND HEALTH

Healthy Living for a Lifetime

When we budget our time, we start by dividing the day into three eight-hour chunks: work, recreation, and sleep. We should keep our health in mind during each of these periods.

At work, we are liable to suffer from stress or overload. We may not be able to change our jobs or the environment where we work, but we can control our reactions and attitudes. Use meditation techniques to handle difficulties. Taking several deep cleansing breaths, for example, can do wonders for relieving stress and anxiety. If you're an office worker, leave your desk occasionally and walk around a bit. Just don't walk over to the vending machine to load up on junk food and soda or coffee. Keep healthy snacks on hand (fruits, vegetables, and nuts) and drink plenty of water. Oftentimes, we confuse thirst with hunger.

Outside of work, on our own time, we can pay more attention to our own needs. The big two needs, of course, are exercise and eating well. There isn't much to add here that you don't already know: 30 minutes of vigorous exercise at least 3 times a week; cut down on sugar, refined foods, caffeine, and alcohol. Get a physical from your physician to find out if you're already suffering from hypertension, high cholesterol, or diabetes, and take the necessary steps to stop these silent killers.

Last, but certainly not least, is sleep. Most of us are chronically sleep-deprived. We need eight hours of rest to recharge both physically and mentally. The best tips I know for better sleep are to keep a regular sleep schedule each night, and to make your bedroom cold and dark. Sleeping well is essential for making the most of your waking hours.

—CHRISTOPHER LAKE

Spaghetti Carbonara

3/4 cup extra virgin olive oil
1/2 pound prosciutto, thinly sliced and cut into 1/8-inch strips widthwise
2 cups dry white wine
3 tablespoons butter
16 ounces spaghetti, cooked al dente
4 egg yolks, whisked together
1 tablespoon fresh ground black pepper

In a large skillet, heat olive oil over medium-high heat. Add prosciutto when oil is hot.

Sauté prosciutto until edges begin to brown.

Deglaze with white wine. When you can smell that most of the alcohol has boiled off (1–2 minutes), reduce heat to medium-low.

Add butter and continue simmering, stirring occasionally, until the sauce begins to thicken.

Remove from heat and add cooked pasta. Toss pasta to coat with sauce.

Add egg yolks and toss again to coat all pasta.

Add fresh ground black pepper liberally to taste. This is a spicy dish. Give pasta one more toss to distribute pepper and dish onto plates or pasta bowls.

Excellent as a meal in itself, or as a side dish.

I am a marketing consultant and writer in Mesa, Arizona. I won't win any bodybuilding contests, but I have learned that eating better, drinking plenty of water (especially here in the desert Southwest), and getting enough sleep are fundamental for good health. When I make an effort to exercise regularly, I have so much more energy for the day. Spending even a brief time out in the sun also invigorates me. Since my work is sedentary, it is even more important that I do something physical every day, whether it is walking the dogs or visiting the gym. I don't always practice what I preach, but I definitely feel the difference when I do. To your health!

Think Globally, Act Locally

My parents brought the values of country living to city life. These are still the wisest principles for sound health: clean air and water, plenty of exercise outdoors in all seasons, fresh fruits and vegetables in season, and a balance of rest and quiet, work, and play. We were instilled with a deep awareness, respect, and reverence for the Creator and all created things. This connection sustains us, invigorates us, revitalizes us, and moves us through the times when health challenges appear. For me, these are still the wisest principles for sound health.

As we become more aware of the implications of our lifestyle, as we grow deeper in the implementation of Napoleon Hill's principles, we become aware of our contributions to the health not only of individuals, but of the entire world. As we come to understand that the food we eat, or the activities we choose, really are our choices for "sound health," we become more empowered to maintain our health. Our choices to reduce the use of chemicals in our diet, in our homes and environment, and in our workplaces not only impact us personally, but also impact the lives of our whole community. Small choices, such as using organically grown produce and humanely raised and slaughtered animals, supporting sustainable agricultural practices, shopping at farmers' markets and smaller family-owned stores, can make such a large difference in the world as we know it. As we become more aware of our connection to the Earth, and our inter-connection with all beings on this planet, we find ways of being more congruent with a life of balance, service, and joy for all people.

—Patsi G.

Tasty Zucchini

Did you ever wonder WHAT to do with all that homegrown zucchini?

   1/2 cup organic sunflower oil (enough to cover the bottom of a 9 to 12 inch frying pan)
   3 medium zucchini cut into 1/2 inch pieces
   7-12 small mushrooms, thin-sliced
   2 large onions, minced
   1 clove garlic, minced
   2 carrots, thin-sliced
   1/2 cup fresh herbs, chopped fine: basil, oregano, parsley, and rosemary, to taste
   1-2 cups parmesan, romano, and mozzarella cheeses, to taste
   1 jar (25 ounces) spaghetti sauce

Heat large frying pan and add oil.

Add zucchini and sauté gently until softened.

Add mushrooms and sauté until softened.

Add onions and garlic. Cook until onions are transparent.

Add carrots, herbs, and spaghetti sauce. Simmer gently for 15 minutes.

Add cheeses. Gently simmer until the mozzarella is melted.

This dish can be served over whole wheat noodles and with a good Italian bread.

My grandfather was a country doctor in a tiny town. My father and mother chose to live in a big city to raise their children. As the daughter of a doctor, and eldest of 24 children, "sound health" underscored every facet of our lives. As a mother, grandmother, and co-owner of a business dedicated to fostering wellness principles in our clients, my lessons growing up in such a large family are precious to me. Welcoming the next generation of grandchildren helps to bring into sharper focus the importance of health in all realms of life.

Recipe Notes:

"Change your mental attitude, and the world around you will change accordingly."

16. Budgeting Time And Money

Dr. Hill states: "Tell me how you use your spare time and how you spend your money, and I will tell you where and what you will be ten years from now." This statement makes many of us cringe because we would rather focus on our best qualities rather than those attributes we are lacking. Budgeting anything often has a negative ring to it. We like to speak of abundance rather than budget because budget implies lack. But, it we change the lens we use to look at life, this budgeting can be a good thing because it enables us to make the best use of our resources without wasting a thing. Waste is not positive. When we waste, we are lacking in gratitude for the gifts we have received. A by-product of abundance should never be waste. The two recipes appearing in this section should create no waste yet budget our time and money in unison. And, your family and guests will surely enjoy them too!

- Judith Williamson

Date Oatmeal Squares

1 c. coarsely chopped dates

½ c. water

1 tsp. vanilla

1 c. rolled oats

½ c. sifted flour

1 tsp. vanilla

½ c. packed brown sugar

½ c. melted margarine or butter

Preheat oven to 350 degrees. Grease an 8x8x2 inch pan. Simmer together chopped dates and water until thickened. Stir in 1 teaspoon vanilla. Set aside. Combine brown sugar, oats and flour. Add butter and vanilla while stirring. Press ½ of oat mixture into bottom of pan. Cover with date mixture, then sprinkle with remaining oatmeal mixture. Pat gently, bake 20 minutes. Cool completely before cutting.

Note: Good and healthy too!

Budgeting Time and Money

> " Tell me how you use your spare time…and…money, and I will tell you where you will be ten years from now. "
> -Napoleon Hill

Recipe for Budgeting Your Time

Experience has proved that the following schedule is one which the majority of people can easily follow. It has also proved that it is an efficient schedule.

- 8 hours for sleep
- 8 hours for one's vocation
- 4 hours for recreation and health
- 2 hours for study and preparation
- 2 hours for extra service for the benefit of others, without pay

----

24 hours

Recipe for a Master Salesman

A Master Salesman is an artist who can paint word-pictures in the hearts of men as skillfully as Rembrandt could blend colors on a canvas. He is an artist who can play a symphony on the human emotions as effectively as Paderewski can manipulate the key of a piano.

A Master Salesman is a strategist at mind manipulation. He can marshal the thoughts of men as ably as Foch directed the allied armies during the World War.

A Master Salesman is a philosopher who can interpret causes by their effects and effects by their causes.

A Master Salesman is a character analyst. He knows men as Einstein knows higher mathematics.

A Master Salesman is a mind-reader. He knows what thoughts are in men's minds by the words they utter, by their silence, and by the "feeling" which he experiences from within, while in their presence.

The Master Salesman is a "Fortune Teller." He can predict the future by observing what has happened in the past.

The Master Salesman is master of others BECAUSE HE IS MASTER OF HIMSELF!

Company Short Ribs with Horseradish Sauce

3 to 5 lbs. short ribs

salt and pepper to taste

1 T. butter

2 large onions, quartered

2 cloves garlic, minced

4 stalks celery, sliced

2 carrots, chopped

1 bay leaf

Brown short ribs in butter in a large frying pan. Add salt and pepper to taste. As they brown, add the two large onions quartered and the minced garlic. Continue to brown for about 7-10 minutes. Remove meat, onions, garlic, plus any drippings to a large crock pot. Cover meat with hot water, add the bay leaf, sliced celery, and chopped carrots. Cook on high 6-8 hours. Add additional water during cooking if necessary to maintain stock.

Sauce 1:

2 ½ c. beef stock

1 c. prepared horseradish

2 egg yolks, well beaten

salt to taste

Prior to serving, remove 2 and ½ cups of the stock. To this, add 1 cup of prepared horseradish and stir in the beaten yolks of 2 eggs. Reheat, but do not boil. Season to taste with salt. Serve sauce separately from the short ribs.

Sauce 2: (my favorite – an old New Orleans recipe)

1 c. prepared horseradish

1 ½ c. tomato ketchup

Mix the two ingredients together and serve on the side.

Note: This dinner is both unusual and good. Can be served with noodles as an accompaniment.

Spare Time

In the past, I thought "spare time" was a funny way of saying "take work home time." After years of never budgeting my spare time, I suddenly found myself bored, boring, tired, disliking my chosen work, and struggling to remember the names of my children! The truth was, how I spent my spare time did not align with my major purpose.

A friend convinced me to read *Think and Grow Rich*. It was an eye opener! I decided that if I could develop a personal purpose in life, then I could change my life and renew my family relationships. I defined a purpose that included family relationship goals as well as professional goals. Having both written down made them easy to review to renew my enthusiasm.

My perspective changed. Spare time became important time. Now an hour meditating on attaining my purpose captures my attention. Accumulating two hours throughout the day going the extra mile for someone else creates joy. Reading for an hour a day in self-improvement books hardly seems enough. Mastermind activity for family or career can fit into the day. Three hours of recreation and relaxation helps renew my spirit daily—it is the color in my fabric of life. The biggest difference is that I am only able to sleep at night if I have planned out the next day to include these activities in addition to my daily occupation.

The key is to budget balance into life. Just like each meal includes a balance of protein, carbohydrates, and healthy fats to keep my body functioning, each day needs to include a healthy balance of sleep time, work time, and spare time, all focused on attaining my definite major purpose.

—Gus Gates

Gail's Chicken Parmesan

- 1/2 teaspoon seasoned salt
- 1/2 teaspoon garlic powder, minced garlic, or crushed garlic pepper (optional)
- 1/2 teaspoon minced onion (optional)
- 1 cup flour
- 4 boneless, skinless chicken breasts
- 1 egg
- 1/3 cup extra virgin olive oil
- 1/4 green pepper, chopped
- 1/4 sweet red pepper, chopped
- 4 baby portabella mushrooms, sliced
- 1 can or jar spaghetti sauce
- 1 cup mozzarella cheese, grated
- 1 pound pasta
- 1/2 cup parmesan cheese, grated

Preheat oven to 350 degrees.

In a zip-top bag, mix seasoned salt, garlic, minced onion, and flour.

In a small bowl, beat the egg. Dip chicken pieces in egg and place in bag. Close the bag and toss the pieces until well covered.

Brown the chicken in olive oil. Remove chicken from pan and place in a greased casserole pan and bake for 30 minutes.

Sauté the mushrooms and peppers in the olive oil until the mushrooms have reduced and the peppers are shiny but still firm. Mix with the spaghetti sauce and pour over the chicken.

Top with grated mozzarella and bake another 30 minutes.

Serve with your choice pasta and grated parmesan cheese.

*A dream that is bigger than who you are now—I believed everyone should have one of these. But, a dream without a way to achieve it is just a dream. When I decided to take time every day to read **Think and Grow Rich**— and then actually to follow through and read it daily—I discovered a way that I could take control of my life. I know now I will achieve the balanced success I dream of.*

Recipe Notes

Andrew Carnegie

17. Cosmic Habitforce

Cosmic Habitforce is said to be the comptroller of the universe. It is the law by which the equilibrium of the universe is maintained through established patterns, or habits of thoughts and deeds. It is the glue that holds the entire philosophy of success together. It is essential to accept the fact that the universe works under undeniable laws, and these laws work to our benefit when we understand them and coordinate our efforts in keeping with their universal truths. Truth is eternal and universal. When we understand this, things become easier to achieve because we are certain of the laws of fulfillment. The mystery is solved and we proceed to our destiny knowing that we are a co-creator of the outcome. However, when things get overwhelming, it is good to know as Norman Cousins tells us, that humor is healing and laughter is spiritual. The soup recipe below is easy and quick to make. The subtitle again comes from my son Tim. He would frequently request Belly Button Soup because it was easy to say and the tortellini resembles belly buttons – at least in his young eyes. In reflecting on this belly button issue, I am reminded that it is not good to spend undue time in contemplating our navels. Little can be gained from this activity. Navel gazers need to become star gazers in order to manifest their destiny. Looking within always leads to looking without if we follow the logical order of things. Next, the potato pancake recipe can be spiritual in nature too. In the Jewish belief system, potato latkes are served during the holiday season. Wouldn't it be a blessing if the best beliefs of all spiritual practices could be internalized as easily as their culinary delights? Anyway, for now Shalom, and Peace be with you too.

- Judith Williamson

Tortellini-Basil Soup
(Belly Button Soup)

4 c. canned chicken broth, undiluted

1 9-oz. fresh cheese-filled tortellini, uncooked

1 15-oz. can cannelloni beans, drained

1 c. chopped tomato

½ c. shredded fresh basil

2 T. balsamic vinegar

¼ tsp. salt

1/3 c. freshly grated Parmesan cheese

1½ tsp. freshly ground pepper

Bring broth to a boil in a large Dutch oven. Add tortellini, and cook 6 minutes or until tender. Sir in beans and tomato. Reduce heat, and simmer 5 minutes or until thoroughly heated. Remove from heat; stir in basil, vinegar, and salt.

Ladle soup into individual bowls; sprinkle evenly with cheese and pepper.

Yield: 7 one-cup servings.

Note: Hearty soup that everyone loves.

Potato Pancakes

Grate 7 or 8 large potatoes (red ones are best)

And one large onion

Add 2 or 3 eggs

About 1 cup flour

Salt to taste

Mix well and drop in hot grease like pancakes.

Crisco in can works well.

Sauce:

1 cup water

½ cup sugar

2 or 3 tablespoons flour

2 tbls. butter

½ tsp. nutmeg

Cook until thick

Serve as a sauce for the pancakes.

Pancakes are also good with sour cream, butter, and applesauce.

Cosmic Habitforce

> " ...is infinite intelligence in operation. It is a sense of order. "
> -Napoleon Hill

Recipe for Planting Your Garden

Every competent farmer understands and makes use of the law of increasing returns. He puts this law into operation in the following manner:

First: He selects soil which is appropriate for the crop which he expects it to yield.

Second: He then prepares this soil by plowing and harrowing and perhaps by fertilization, so it will be favorable to the seed he plants.

Third: He plants seed which have been carefully selected for soundness, knowing that poor seed cannot yield a bountiful crop.

Fourth: He then gives Nature a chance to compensate him for his labor through an appropriate period of time. He does not sow the seed one day and expect to reap a harvest the next.

Benefits from Cosmic Habitforce

First of all, you should know that this law is the climax of the entire philosophy of individual achievement. To get a slight degree of understanding of the importance of this law, consider the fact that it is the Master Key to the principles previously described, and its benefits are available only to those who master and apply the instructions in previous chapters.

Understanding and application of the law can release you from fears and self-imposed limitations, thus enabling you to take full possession of your own mind!

If it offered no further promise, this would be sufficient to justify all the time you may devote to its study.

It can help you attain economic freedom for life provided you follow the instructions in the previous chapters.

It can aid you in eliminating the opposition of others in all your relationships, thus enabling you to negotiate your way through life with a minimum of friction.

It can help you master most, if not all, of the major causes of physical conditions that cause illness and disease.

It can clear your mind of negative conditions, thus paving the way for that state of mind known as faith.

Cosmic Habit-force is the particular application of energy with which nature maintains the existing relationship between the atoms of matter, the stars and planets, the season of the year, night and day, sickness and health, life and death, and more important to us right now, it is the medium through which all habits and all human relationships are maintained, the medium through which thought is translated into its physical equivalent.

You, of course, know that nature maintains a perfect balance between all the elements of matter and energy throughout the universe. You can see the stars and planets move with perfect precision, each keeping its own place in Time and Space, year in and year out.

You can see the seasons of the year come and go with perfect regularity.

You can see that night and day follow each other in unending regularity.

You can see that an oak tree grows from an acorn and a pine grows from the seed of its ancestor. An acorn never produces a pine nor does a pine cone ever produce an oak, and nothing is ever produced that does not have its antecedents in something else which preceded it.

These are simple facts that anyone can see, but what most people cannot see or understand is the universal law through which nature maintains perfect balance between all matter and energy throughout the universe, forcing every living thing to reproduce itself.

Music is What Feelings Sound Like

I love music. I really feel that the type of music you listen to can put you in the mood you want to be in—especially those favorite tracks you have that get you smiling, and the ones that spark memories of great times in your life. What if you just listened to sad songs all the time for a week? Can you imagine what sort of week you would have, and how your mind and attitude would be affected?

One of the best success recipes is to listen to music and get in touch with Cosmic Habitforce. Man is the only living creature equipped with the power of choice, through which he may establish his own thought and behavior patterns. All the time we have thoughts entering our mind, and we can select the ones we recognize and act upon.

I can share with you that when you listen to good uplifting music, ideas come into your mind with passion. When I have a speech to give, or I need new ideas for my e-zine, or some other challenge facing me, I listen to music and positive ideas start flowing through my mind. It's fantastic and it works.

You only need two ingredients when facing a challenge: something you want to achieve, and a selection of your favorite music. Mix these together and you'll have Cosmic Habitforce in action. Napoleon Hill said you can do it if you believe you can; this recipe will give you the belief. That's a fact!

—CARL GARWOOD

Bangers and Mash

A great traditional British dish.

- 8 large baking potatoes, peeled and quartered
- 2 teaspoons butter, divided
- 1/2 cup milk, or as needed
- salt and pepper to taste
- 1-1/2 pounds beef sausage
- 1/2 cup diced onion
- 1 package (3/4 ounce) dry brown gravy mix
- 1 cup water, or as needed

Preheat the oven to 350 degrees.

Place potatoes in a saucepan with enough water to cover. Bring to a boil, and cook until tender, about 20 minutes. Drain, and mash with 1 teaspoon of butter and enough milk to reach your desired creaminess. Continue mashing, or beat with an electric mixer, until smooth. Season with salt and pepper.

In a large skillet over medium heat, cook the sausage until heated through. Remove from pan and set aside.

Add remaining teaspoon of butter to the skillet, and fry the onions over medium heat until tender. Mix gravy mix and water as directed on the package, and add to the skillet with the onions. Simmer, stirring constantly, to form a thick gravy.

Pour half the gravy into a 9-inch square casserole dish so that it coats the bottom. Place sausages in a layer over the gravy (you can butterfly the sausages if you wish). Pour remaining gravy over them, then top with mashed potatoes.

Bake uncovered for 20 minutes, or until potatoes are evenly brown.

Since I read **Think and Grow Rich** *and took the Science of Success Home Study Course, I have become a leader in my workplace, bought our first dream home, and placed my first book with Amazon and Barnes and Noble. All this thanks to the 17 success principles. My best ideas I have had came to me while listening to music, out of nowhere. Once you have the ideas, you visualize them happening: listen to music and play over and over again in your mind yourself achieving all your goals. It is absolutely true: what the mind can conceive and believe, it can achieve. I wish you all health, happiness, and success. May your dreams come true.*

Increase Happiness Through Cosmic Habitforce

In 2006, I decided to create more happiness for myself and others. I decided to achieve that goal by making the tapestry of my life more beautiful and balanced, both personally and professionally. I decided to follow Dr. Hill's principle of Cosmic Habitforce to do it. I used Cosmic Habitforce to clarify my goals and create plans to achieve them. I developed positive mental habits. I believed in my goals and my ability to follow the path to reach them. I constantly reinforced my beliefs and actions though self discipline and personal initiative.

I have been able to work with people in, and associated with, the Napoleon Hill Foundation in Japan, Malaysia, and the United States. With their support and guidance, in May 2007, I became a certified instructor of the Napoleon Hill Foundation. Now I am prepared to pursue my professional goal of spreading Dr. Hill's philosophy through Canada and Japan.

My husband and I made our dream come true with a romantic wedding in Canada in July 2007. Now we are building our beautiful family life together.

I suggest that you can also make a more beautiful and balanced tapestry in your life by using the power of Cosmic Habitforce. Here is my recipe.

Create a clear vision and goals. "See" your vision and goals achieved in your imagination. Believe that you will achieve your vision and goals. Take steps to reach your goals. Be positively enthusiastic to follow your path. Use self-discipline to help reinforce your habits. Build harmony by following the "Golden Rule": do to and for others what you would like them to do to and for you!

—AYAMI MCARTHUR

Salmon Ravioli

- 3/4 pound fresh, wild salmon, skinned and boned
- 1 package frozen spinach, thawed and pressed to remove water
- 1/8 cup cream
- 1 egg yolk
- 1 pinch nutmeg
- salt and freshly ground pepper to taste
- 5 four-inch wide sheets fresh lasagna pasta
- 2 tablespoons grated parmesan cheese
- 4 cups canned whole tomatoes, coarsely chopped
- 2 medium onions, peeled and cut in half
- 6 tablespoons butter
- 1/2 teaspoon dried basil

In a food processor, blend salmon and spinach until smooth. Transfer the mixture to a bowl and add cream, egg yolk, grated cheese, nutmeg, salt, and pepper. Mix to thoroughly combine.

Place teaspoon-sized scoops of filling 2 inches apart near the center of the lasagna sheets. Moisten pasta edges and between scoops with water. Fold the pasta to cover the scoops. Pinch edges to seal. Cut between the scoops to make individual ravioli packets. Pinch cut edges to seal them too.

Put tomatoes, butter, basil, salt, and onion halves in a saucepan. Bring to boil, then immediately lower heat. Simmer, stirring occasionally. After 30 minutes or so, the tomatoes will start to separate from the butter. Remove from heat. Reserve the onions and serve on the side.

Add ravioli to boiling water and stir. Cook about 3 minutes until al dente. The ravioli is usually ready when it floats. Drain ravioli and place in the saucepan to coat with sauce. Transfer to plates to serve.

When I was younger I had a vision of studying abroad to build my professional skills and enable me to contribute to society with a balanced, holistic approach. I traveled to Carmel, California, to study and work. I was young and knew little, and couldn't speak English well. However, I truly believed that with faith and work my vision would come true. After studying a year in California, I decided to set up a holistic aromatherapy studio. Sometimes it seemed impossible, but the impossible came true. "Coincidences" arose in my life and I was able to establish my studio in a beautiful wellness center in Carmel—exactly the type of place I had foreseen.

COSMIC HABITFORCE

Nuts Know How

Napoleon Hill defines Cosmic Habitforce as pertaining to the universe as a whole and the laws that govern it. Cosmic Habitforce is Infinite Intelligence in operation with a sense of order. Developing positive, constructive habits, including thought habits as well as habits of action, grows a person to unbelievable heights. Just as a nut (acorn) has within it the blueprint to become a mighty oak tree, so does a person's subconscious mind know how to tap into Infinite Intelligence, by understanding that it is "a part of and the same as" and not apart from that force.

A seed does not deviate from the master plan for its growth and perfection. Working with the laws of the universe yields success. Trying to alter those laws ends in failure. Nature demands harmony and harmony of thought energy combined with proper action produces a perfect desired result every time.

—JAMES SPOONER

"The orderliness of the world gives evidence that all natural laws are under the control of a universal plan."

"All voluntary positive habits are the products of will power directed toward the attainment of definite goals."

— NAPOLEON HILL

Glazed Pecans

3 cups unsalted pecans
2 egg whites
1 cup granulated sugar
1 dash salt
1/2 cup butter

Preheat oven to 325 degrees.

Melt butter in 9-inch by 12-inch baking dish.

Combine egg whites, sugar, and salt, and beat until stiff.

Add pecans to egg white mixture and stir until pecans are thoroughly covered.

Add to melted butter and stir.

Bake at 325 degrees for 30 minutes, stirring every 10 minutes.

Spread on wax paper to cool.

Note: there will be a lot of crumbs which may be kept for topping ice cream, pies, etc.

As a teenager I was introduced to Hill's philosophy and put it to the test at an early age. I stood outside a boarded-up 30,000 square foot building containing an empty swimming pool and took possession of it in my mind. An idea was planted deep within my subconscious mind to bring the building back to life. With no money, only faith in the universe, I waited for a plan to come to me. Within seven days, my purpose and future had been cast and the Bentley Club was born. A unique athletic and self-improvement complex grew before my eyes over 18 years, and thousands of lives were enhanced because I understood the nature of an orderly universe.

Napoleon Hill Tossed Salad

Mix:

2 parts definiteness of purpose, as a basis for the salad

1 part applied faith

1 part going the extra mile

1 part pleasing personality

1 part personal initiative

1 part positive mental attitude

1 part enthusiasm

1 part self discipline

1 part accurate thinking

1 part controlled attention

1 part teamwork

1 part creative vision

1 part budgeting and money

Sprinkle liberally with:

— learning from adversity and defeat

— sound health

— cosmic habitforce

Carefully toss and provide generous helpings. Ingredients may be increased or modified when necessary.

—JUDITH B. ARCY

Vegetable Salad

1 large can (22 ounces) green beans, drained
1 can (14 ounces) yellow beans, drained
1 can (14 ounces) kidney beans, drained
1 can (14 ounces) hominy, drained
1 onion, chopped
1 green bell pepper, chopped
4 stalks celery, chopped
1 pimento, chopped
1/2 cup salad oil
1/2 cup water
1/2 cup vinegar
1 cup sugar
1 tablespoon salt
1 teaspoon pepper
1 teaspoon paprika

In a large bowl, mix beans, hominy, onion, bell pepper, celery, and pimento.

In a small bowl, whip oil, water, vinegar, sugar, salt, pepper, and paprika into a dressing.

Add dressing to the vegetables. Toss thoroughly. Let stand at least 2 hours, preferably overnight.

Last year I retired from my "professional career." Although I had some vague plans for what I wanted to accomplish during the next phase of my life, I wanted to stay flexible and be ready for new adventures and choices. That's when Napoleon Hill, via Judy Williamson, came into my life. As an educator, both in the public sector and for the Department of the Navy, I had always been aware of the importance of enhancing the individual talents of my students, yet I also had the pleasure of seeing how often they were able to accomplish wonderful things as a group. I have found the same pleasure in my association with the Napoleon Hill Foundation.

COSMIC HABITFORCE

The Blend

As I started to read and understand Napoleon Hill's 17 principles, I had no idea how much they would become a part of my life. Like any recipe, each ingredient lends itself to the whole without giving itself totally up. Each principle likewise lends itself to the whole without giving itself totally up.

I didn't gain this understanding until I started applying the 17 principles to my life. I didn't have the foggiest idea how I was ever going to fit all these things into my life, until the universe handed me the moment: I was hospitalized with a partially blocked bowel which turned into a diagnosis of cancer. Surgery and its recovery, with some complications, took care of the cancer. As I lay in the hospital bed, I had more than adequate time to reflect on each of the principles and how they had and continued to influence my life.

Definiteness of purpose, positive mental attitude, applied faith, learning from adversity and defeat—the principles were all there, each to be used individually when needed or blended together as a whole. Prayer, meditation, relaxation, and reading and writing were a few of the tools I used during recovery. Then the next treatment began: chemotherapy.

Chemo continued once a week for six months. And once again, there were the 17 principles, right along with me. There were moments when I would ask myself, "What am I doing?" and there it was: my definiteness of purpose would pop into my mind, followed by applied faith, and so it goes, even today. Each of the 17 principles influences my life and "The Blend" makes me a better person, yearning to share with others.

—MICHAEL FRAIN

Noodle Candy

2 packages (14 ounces each) semisweet chocolate chips
1 package (14 ounces) butterscotch chips
1 can (22 ounces) chow mein noodles

In a double boiler over low to medium heat, melt the chocolate chips.

When the chocolate is almost completely melted, add the butterscotch chips and stir with a wooden spoon.

Continue stirring until completely melted and blended.

Remove candy from heat and stir in chow mein noodles.

Once the noodles are blended and the mix begins to set, drop by teaspoonfuls onto wax paper.

Let cool completely, then enjoy.

I came into this reality on a dark and stormy October night. Interestingly, I kept my life dark and stormy for many years. Fears, self-doubt, self-hatred, and lack of purpose were the predominant motivators in my life. It wasn't until I found myself a single parent of four, a full-time employee, and a "recovering person" that pinholes of light started to penetrate my darkness. For years I have participated in processes and programs that help people. This includes teaching Dr. Hill's principles to young people who are incarcerated. The last four years of my life have been trying, but this has taught me that the application of all 17 principles is a powerful blend.

The Perfect Recipe for Positive Change

I was born in Chicago. and at the age of 17, as a result of some poor choices and bad decisions that I had made, I was shot. At that time, I realized I had a second chance at life and I knew that if I didn't get out of Chicago there would be a very good chance that I would end up dead or in jail. At 18, I packed up what few belongings I had and moved to Southern California to start a new life. I took a sales position with a company and was introduced to **Think and Grow Rich**. Somehow I had managed to graduate from high school without ever reading a book, and **Think and Grow Rich** became the first book that I ever read.

To say that the book helped me to transform my life would be an understatement. It not only helped me transform my life, it helped transform all of the relationships with all the people around me. Over the last 30 years, I have used all of the 17 principles to become successful in business, to overcome adversity (a bankruptcy and the death of my wife when I was 26), and to develop self-discipline and a positive mental attitude.

The 17 principles are so powerful that they even work if you don't know about them. I mention this, because before I read the book, I had a definiteness of purpose: to get out of Chicago and better myself. The real turning point was learning about positive mental attitude. When I changed my attitude, everything around me changed. It was then I realized that the only person I had the power to change is myself, and when I change, everything around me changes. Amazing how my life changed by putting Dr. Hill's principles to work.

—DAN GIBBONS

Pasta e Fagioli Italian Soup

1 lb. lean ground beef
1 small onion, diced
1 large carrot, julienned
3 stalks celery, chopped
2 cloves garlic, minced
2 14.5-oz. cans diced tomatoes
1 15-oz. can red kidney beans with liquid
1 15-oz. can great northern beans with liquid
1 15-oz can tomato sauce
1 12-oz can V-8 juice
1 T. white vinegar
1½ tsp. salt
1 tsp. oregano
1 tsp. basil
½ tsp. pepper
½ teaspoon thyme
½ lb. ditali pasta

Brown the ground beef in a large saucepan or pot over medium heat. Drain off most of the fat.

Add onion, carrot, celery and garlic and sauté for 10 minutes.

Add remaining ingredients, except pasta, and simmer for 1 hour.

About 50 minutes into simmer time, cook the pasta in 1½ to 2 quarts of boiling water over high heat. Cool for 10 minutes or just until pasta is al dente, or slightly tough. Drain.

Add the pasta to the large pot of soup. Simmer for 5-10 minutes and serve.

Serves 8.

Note: Very authentic and simple to make. Serve with crusty bread and a glass of wine!

I was born in Chicago, Illinois, and graduated from high school in 1976. I currently run a successful marketing company in Denver, Colorado. I have also been involved in personal development and leadership training for 20 years. I'm married to my wife, Jean, and have 2 boys, ages 18 and 6. I am proud that I use my talents and gifts to make a positive difference in the world with as many people as I possibly can.

Recipe Notes:

_____
_____
_____
_____
_____
_____
_____
_____
_____
_____
_____
_____
_____
_____
_____
_____
_____
_____
_____
_____
_____
_____
_____
_____

"Control your own mind, and you may never be controlled by the mind of another."

Recipe for Success

My Daily Success Creed
by Napoleon Hill

1. I know that I have the ability to achieve the object of my definite major purpose in life: Therefore I DEMAND of myself, persistent, continuous action toward its attainment, and I here and now promise to render such action.

2. I realize the dominating thoughts of my mind will eventually reproduce themselves in outward, physical action, and gradually transform themselves into physical reality: Therefore, I will concentrate my thoughts for thirty minutes daily upon the task of thinking of the person I intend to become, thereby creating in my mind a clear mental picture of that person.

3. I know that through the principle of auto-suggestion, any desire I persistently hold in my mind will eventually seek expression through some practical means of attaining the object back of it: Therefore, I will devote ten minutes daily to demanding of myself the development of unconditional self-reliance.

4. I have clearly written down a description of my definite chief aim in life, and I will never stop trying until I shall have developed sufficient self-reliance for its attainment in full.

5. I fully realize that no wealth or position of benefit can long endure, unless built upon truth and justice: Therefore, I will engage in no transaction, in no human relationship, which does not benefit all whom it affects. I will succeed by attracting to myself the forces I wish to use, and the co-operation of other people. I will induce others to serve me, because of willingness to serve others. I will eliminate hatred, envy, jealousy, selfishness, greed and cynicism, by developing love for all humanity, because I know that a negative mental attitude toward others can never bring me success. I will cause others to believe in me, because I will believe in them, and in myself.

I will sign my name to this formula, commit it to memory, and repeat it aloud at least once daily, with full faith that it will gradually influence my thoughts and actions so that I will become self-reliant and successful.

Signed: _____

(This should be read morning, noon, and night. When signed, it creates a contract with yourself for individual success.)

Contributors

Recipes by Napoleon Hill

Principle	Recipe	Page
Definiteness of Purpose	Recipe for Success	2
	Recipe for a Definite Major Purpose	2
Mastermind Alliance	Recipe for Success – Compact with Invisible Princes	10
	Recipe for a Mastermind – Compact with Yourself	11
Applied Faith	Recipe for Hope and Promise	18
	Recipe for Faith	19
Going The Extra Mile	Recipe for the Habit of Doing More	30
	Recipe for Attracting Attention by Going the Extra Mile	31
Pleasing Personality	Recipe for Developing Self-Confidence	40
	Recipe for an Attractive Personality	41
Personal Initiative	Recipe for Goal Setting	46
	Recipe for the Development of Leadership	47
Positive Mental Attitude	Recipe for Controlling Your Mental Attitude	52
Enthusiasm	Recipe for Speaking Enthusiastically	62
	Recipe for Inspiring Enthusiasm	63
Self-Discipline	Recipe for Fighting Pessimism	70
	Recipe Ingredients for Personal Power	70
Accurate Thinking	Recipe for Reading a Self-Help Book Accurately	76
Controlled Attention	Recipe for a Supercharged Success Formula	80
	Recipes for Microwaves	80
Teamwork	Recipe for Teamwork	86
	Recipe for Beneficial Teamwork	87
Learning From Adversity And Defeat	Recipe for Getting Rid of Guilt	92
	Recipe for Life	93
Creative Vision	Recipe for Ideas	102
	Recipe Ingredients for Imagination	102
Maintenance Of Sound Health	Recipe for Solitude	108
	Recipe for Mental Equipment	109
Budgeting Time And Money	Recipe for Budgeting Your Time	114
	Recipe for a Master Salesman	114
Cosmic Habitforce	Recipe for Planting Your Garden	120
	Recipe for Benefiting from Cosmic Habitforce	121

Recipes Submitted by Judith Wiliamson

Principle	Recipe	Page
Definiteness of Purpose	Lone Ranger Soup	1
	Icebox Cheese Cake – Old Fashioned	3
Mastermind Alliance	Chicken Tortilla Soup	9
	Heavenly Fluff	9
Applied Faith	Bacon Wraps	17
	Baked Mushrooms	17
Going The Extra Mile	Snowballs	29
	Homestead Spice Cookies	29
Pleasing Personality	Carolina Cole Slaw	39
	Rosy Glow Punch	39
Personal Initiative	Nut Rolls	45
	Poteca	48
Positive Mental Attitude	Marshmallow Fruit Salad	51
	Bread Pudding with Whiskey Sauce	51
Enthusiasm	Deviled Eggs	61
	Festive Fruit Cake	64
Self-Discipline	Pineapple Upside-Down Cake	69
	Apple Dumplings	69
Accurate Thinking	Tuna Casserole	75
	Holiday Ham	75
Controlled Attention	Classic Pot Roast	79
	Meat Loaf	79
Teamwork	Juanita's Special Chicken Salad	85
	Hobo Dinner	85
Learning From Adversity And Defeat	Cowboy Beans	91
	Corned Beef Hash Patties	91
Creative Vision	Cincinnati 5-Way Chili	101
	Nut Tarts	101
Maintenance Of Sound Health	Cole Slaw	107
	Jell-O with Fruit	107
Budgeting Time And Money	Date Oatmeal Squares	113
	Company Short Ribs with Horseradish Sauce	115
Cosmic Habitforce	Tortellini-Basil Soup	119
	Potato Pancakes	119

Email Judith Williamson at: nhf@purduecal.edu

Last/First Name	Principle	Recipe	Page
Alperstein, Eliezer A.	Going The Extra Mile	Sweet Whole Wheat Challah	32
Aminaka, Tatsuya	Going The Extra Mile	Aminaka's Sukiyaki	33
Arcy, Judith B.	Cosmic Habitforce	Vegetable Salad	125
Arnold, Marie	Mastermind Alliance	Veggie Lasagna	12
Banta, Richard	Accurate Thinking	Brilliant Tacos	77
Barlow, Phil	Positive Mental Attitude	Best Ever Chicken Salad	54
Brooks, Gail	Learning From Adversity	Chocolate Chip Cake	94
Byrd, Diane Marie	Personal Initiative	Sauerkraut, Kielbasa, and Potato Noodles	49
Campbell, Raymond	Mastermind Alliance	Michigan White Bean Chicken Chili	13
Chen, Guang "Alan"	Positive Mental Attitude	Tofu Balls	55
Chia, Christina	Applied Faith	Szechuan Hot and Sour Soup	20
Connelly, Jim	Definiteness of Purpose	Donna's Italian Beef with Manicotti	7
Dunkerton, Martin	Applied Faith	Chicken With Many Cloves of Garlic	21
Frain, Michael	Cosmic Habitforce	Noodle Candy	126
Freireich, Gary	Controlled Attention	German Potato Salad	82
G., Patsi	Maintenance Of Sound Health	Tasty Zucchini	111
Garwood, Carl	Cosmic Habitforce	Bangers and Mash	122
Gates, Gus	Budgeting Time and Money	Gail's Chicken Parmesan	116
Gibbons, Dan	Cosmic Habitforce	Pasta e Fagioli Italian Soup	127
Gill, Mel	Definiteness of Purpose	African Prawn Salad	4
Grant, Stephen	Pleasing Personality	Southern Shrimp & Grits	42
Hershberger, Nina	Mastermind Alliance	Corn Casserole	14
Jackson, Wilma	Positive Mental Attitude	Mrs. Sees' Fudge	56
Jarvis, Rebecca	Applied Faith	Amish Friendship Bread Starter	22
Jones, Maryann W.	Applied Faith	Italian Beef	23
Kapoor, Rajiv	Positive Mental Attitude	Benarsi Thandai (Indian Dry-Fruit Drink)	57
Krasney, Richard J.	Definiteness of Purpose	Passion Fruit Syrup	5
Lake, Christopher	Maintenance Of Sound Health	Spaghetti Carbonara	110
Lake, Laura Dietrich	Learning From Adversity	Mango Pineapple Salsa	95
Larsen, Gaynell M.	Enthusiasm	Gay Gay's Orzo Salad	65
Lee, George	Positive Mental Attitude	Bo Bo Cha Cha	58
Levin, Loretta	Going The Extra Mile	Migas	37
Lutton, Cheri	Creative Vision	Shrimp Pasta Primavera	104
Madrano, Sheryn	Teamwork	Steamed Tilapia	88
Martinez, Uriel "Chino"	Creative Vision	Ofelia's Mexican Rice	103
McArthur, Ayami	Cosmic Habitforce	Salmon Ravioli	123
McCauley, Philip	Going The Extra Mile	Traditional Irish Stew	34
McClean, Boyd	Controlled Attention	Toffee & English Toffee	81
Naifeh, Dee	Applied Faith	Waikiki Chicken	24
Peterson, Audra	Teamwork	Artichoke Dip	89
Sikorski, Donna Green	Creative Vision	Tilapia with Lemon Vinaigrette	105
Spooner, James	Cosmic Habitforce	Glazed Pecans	124
Sturgill, Annedia	Applied Faith	Cheese Ball	26
Tan, Juan Keat	Going The Extra Mile	Soy Milk	35
Upton, Robin J.	Definiteness of Purpose	Aunt Ruthie's Yummy Blueberry Cake	6
Vitale, Emiliano	Applied Faith	Nonna's Spaghetti Napolitana	25
Ward, Virginia C.	Self-Discipline	Arroz Con Leche (Rice with Milk)	71
Washausen, Gayle	Enthusiasm	Aunt Rose's Yum-Yum Coffee Cake	66
Watkins, Allen	Learning From Adversity	Hershey's Chocolate Barbecue Sauce	98
Watkins, Debra T.	Learning From Adversity	Lemon Basil Halibut	96
Wein, Lisa	Learning From Adversity	Barley and Mushroom Casserole	97
Wikkeling, Fred	Positive Mental Attitude	Pound Cake	59
Williamson, Cathleen	Self-Discipline	Vegetarian Cheesy Lasagna	72
Wright, Rose	Going The Extra Mile	Delicious Grape Salad	36
Yap, Poly	Pleasing Personality	Simple and Nutritious Toaster Oven Chicken	43

Last/First Name	Email	Article Title	Page
Alperstein, Eliezer A.	eliealp@zahav.net.il	Your Number One Competitive Advantage	32
Aminaka, Tatsuya	aminakapmadream@u01.gate01.com	A Recipe as Simple as QQS	33
Arcy, Judith B.	judyarcy@bellsouth.net	Napoleon Hill Tossed Salad	125
Arnold, Marie	marnold@lightstreampublishing.com	Hang in There! Some Things Just Take Time	12
Banta, Richard	rbantaatty@earthlink.net	Accurate Thinking is Critical for Success	77
Barlow, Phil	Phil.Barlow@shawinc.com	Positivity is Infectious	54
Brooks, Gail	gail1@netexpress.net	The Turning Point	94
Byrd, Diane Marie	jebyrdnest@comcast.net	Achieve Your Dreams	49
Campbell, Raymond	rcampbell@us-net.com	The Positive You	13
Chen, Guang "Alan"	guangc@hotmail.com	You Can Choose Your Life	55
Chia, Christina	christinachia@napoleonhill.com.my	Impossible or Incredible?	20
Connelly, Jim	jcnd@comcast.net	Just One More Sunset	7
Dunkerton, Martin	creationfilms@hotmail.com	Awaken Your Secret	21
Frain, Michael	frainm52@hotmail.com	The Blend	126
Freireich, Gary	hydrmn@msn.com	Keep Your Mind on the Things You Want...	82
G., Patsi	pbgately@comcast.net	Think Globally, Act Locally	111
Garwood, Carl	mail@carlgarwood.com	Music is What Feelings Sound Like	122
Gates, Gus	gusgates@comcast.net	Spare Time	116
Gibbons, Dan	dan@dvgibbons.com	The Perfect Recipe for Positive Change	127
Gill, Mel	drmelgill@gmail.com	S.M.A.R.T.E.R. Than You Think	4
Grant, Stephen	sgrant2544@verizon.net	Southern Hospitality: A Form of a Pleasing...	42
Hershberger, Nina	nina@megabucksmarketing.com	Establish a Mastermind Alliance	14
Jackson, Wilma	wilmajacksonhome@aol.com	Simple Recipe for Happiness	56
Jarvis, Rebecca	jarvisbl@hotmail.com	Progress Through Faith	22
Jones, Maryann W.	marinerparent@prodigy.net	Applied Faith Will Get You Through	23
Kapoor, Rajiv	raj_a2in@yahoo.co.in	Win The World In Three Steps	57
Krasney, Richard J.	rkrasney@rjkwealth.com	A Purposeful Lifetime Relationship with Wealth	5
Lake, Christopher	cmlake@cmlstudios.com	Healthy Living for a Lifetime	110
Lake, Laura Dietrich	cmlake@cmlstudios.com	Planting Seeds of Opportunity	95
Larsen, Gaynell M.	dlarsen@swva.net	The Fuel that Creates Momentum	65
Lee, George	anneyct@yahoo.com	Switch to Your Positive Self	58
Levin, Loretta	Loretta@levineyecare.com	A Sweet Recipe for Sweet Success	37
Lutton, Cheri	cherilutton@ccgh.com	Trusting in Your Dreams	104
Madrano, Sheryn	creationfilms@hotmail.com	A Family Team	88
Martinez, Uriel "Chino"	martineu@calumet.purdue.edu	A Recipe for Creative Vision	103
McArthur, Ayami	ayamimcarthur@hotmail.com	Increase Happiness Through Cosmic Habitforce	123
McCauley, Philip	philmc40@hotmail.com	Walk Awhile with Me!	34
McClean, Boyd	boydmcclean@hotmail.com	Persistence Pays Off	81
Naifeh, Dee	nafe51@comcast.net	Summon Applied Faith	24
Peterson, Audra	alpeterson@hammond.k12.in.us	My Element of Success	89
Sikorski, Donna Green	dgsikorski@bvunet.net	Just Imagine	105
Spooner, James	bentleylabs@aol.com	Nuts Know How	124
Sturgill, Annedia	napoleonhill@uvawise.edu	Applied Faith and Teamwork Lead to Success	26
Tan, Juan Keat	leben104@singnet.com.sg	Do You Have that Something Extra?	35
Upton, Robin J.	rupton@mcsquared.org	Believe and You Shall Receive!	6
Vitale, Emiliano	emilianohairguru@aol.com	When You Dream and Believe, You Will Achieve	25
Ward, Virginia C.	virginiacward@cox.net	To Grow Daily	71
Washausen, Gayle	washause@calumet.purdue.edu	Parenting with Enthusiasm	66
Watkins, Allen	allenwatkins@yahoo.com	Never, Never, Never, Never, Never Give Up!	98
Watkins, Debra T.	allenwatkins@yahoo.com	Learning From Adversity and Defeat Brings...	96
Wein, Lisa	havenhouseDVS@aol.com	Adversity is Like an Onion	97
Wikkeling, Fred	smsiexit@gmail.com	Positive Mental Attitude Creates Positive Lives	59
Williamson, Cathleen	irishcaitland@yahoo.com	Direct Your Thoughts...Ordain Your Destiny	72
Wright, Rose	wrightwr@comcast.net	Better to Give than Receive	36
Yap, Poly	polyap@pc.jaring.my	First Impressions are Lasting	43

Dear Reader,

Napoleon Hill's Cookbook for Life: The Magic Ingredients of Success, 2nd edition is in the works and I would like you to donate a success recipe and a food recipe for inclusion in our next edition. Considering that there are 17 success principles, I would like your recipe for success to align with one of the principles which you name, and next I would like you to outline a brief "recipe" that you use to bring this principle to life. For example, if you select Enthusiasm you would then tell the reader about your "recipe" for creating enthusiasm in your life.

Next, you would contribute your best ever food recipe that will wake up our taste buds just like your success recipe wakes up our life! This book will feature food for our body and food for our soul!

Also, I will need a good head and shoulders shot of you – your choice – to be included on the page with a paragraph of personal information of your own choosing. Interspersed throughout the book will be "recipes" by Dr. Hill that tell the reader how to achieve whatever it is he or she wants in life. The recipe link is below, and you must add the recipes right on the page. Photo can be sent to me as an attachment at the bottom of the page after you hit the submit button. In these days of digital photography, getting a good image is easy. Practice until you get one that you like!

Submit your recipes via this link `http://www.cmlstudios.com/recipes.php`

You can also view sample mock-up pages at this link.

I would like to thank you for participating in this project free of charge. All submissions become the property of the Napoleon Hill Foundation. It's fun to see yourself and your ideas in print. Your reward will come in good karma that is being sent to you for making the world a better place in which to live one single thought (recipe) at a time!

I thoroughly appreciate your help and dedication to the mission of the Napoleon Hill Foundation.

Judy Williamson

17 Principles of Success

Definiteness of Purpose, Mastermind Alliance, Applied Faith, Going the Extra Mile, Pleasing Personality, Personal Initiative, Positive Mental Attitude, Enthusiasm, Self-Discipline, Accurate Thinking, Controlled Attention, Teamwork, Learning from Adversity and Defeat, Creative Vision, Maintenance of Sound Health, Budgeting Time and Money, and Cosmic Habitforce.

Note: Submission of content for publication implies the transfer of the copyright from the author to the Publisher upon acceptance. Accepted content becomes the permanent property of ***The Napoleon Hill Foundation*** and may not be reproduced by any means, in whole or in part, without the written consent of the Publisher.

Positive Mental Attitude: A System of Self Management

A Distance Learning Class licensed by the Napoleon Hill Foundation.

Non-Credit Course: Tuition - $599.00

This online distance learning course presents and examines the principles of success researched and developed by Dr. Napoleon Hill and others. It provides a framework for students to better understand life's opportunities and the need for definiteness of purpose. The class is based on and structured around Hill's 17 Principles of Success. Each lesson focuses on one principle and contains online reading assignments, points to ponder, chapter quizzes, vintage audio, articles form the **Think and Grow Rich** and *PMA Advisor* newsletter, discussion group, journal assignments and activities, and a class forum. Each student in the class has a personalized relationship with a fully accredited and approved instructor for Napoleon Hill Distance Learning Courses. The class concludes with an assignment dealing with an individualized plan for personal success.

To apply:

Log on to www.naphill.org

Or email:

nhf@purduecal.edu

You may also call (219) 989-3173 or (219) 989-3166

Our mailing address:

Napoleon Hill World Learning Center

Purdue University Calumet

2300 173rd Street

Hammond, IN 46323-2094

As the Napoleon Hill World Learning Center at Purdue University Calumet, our goal is to disseminate Napoleon Hill's works to all audiences that are open and interested. Currently, our focus is on the general student and correctional populations nationwide. Youth and adult programs are available as specially arranged seminars as well. Instructors in your area are available to work within your budget and program requirements. For special requests, please contact us at nhf@purduecal.edu.

Also Available From the Napoleon Hill World Learning Center:

BOOKS

Think and Grow Rich

Yearly Inspirational Calendar

You Can

Your Greatest Power

How to Become a Mental Millionaire

Timeless Thoughts for Today

Wake Up! You're Alive

Beyond Positive Thinking

Making Miracles

52 Lessons for Life

Paloma

COURSES

PMA - Science of Success Course - Home Study Kit

PMA - Distance Learning Course - (Keys to Success)

Leader Certification Seminar

Beginner, Intermediate, and Advanced Programs
For the 17 Success Principles - Instructor Led

Prison Population Courses

Correctional Courses and Materials Nationwide
For incarcerated youth and adults

Domestic Violence Center Programs

Membership

Mastermind Online at www.naphill.org

Website

www.naphill.org